Our World Tomorrow

How technology will change our lives

英語で学ぶ地球の未来とSDGs

Adam Murray
Anderson Passos

NAN'UN-DO

Download Audio

音声ファイル
無料 DL
のご案内

このテキストの音声を無料で視聴（ストリーミング）・ダウンロードできます。自習用音声としてご活用ください。
以下のサイトにアクセスしてテキスト番号で検索してください。

https://nanun-do.com　テキスト番号［ **512207** ］

※ 無線 LAN（WiFi）に接続してのご利用を推奨いたします。

※ 音声ダウンロードは Zip ファイルでの提供になります。
お使いの機器によっては別途ソフトウェア（アプリケーション）の導入が必要となります。

※ Our World Tomorrow 音声ダウンロードページは以下の QR コードからもご利用になれます。

Read by

Anya Floris
Chris Koprowski

Our World Tomorrow
How technology will change our lives

About this book

Our World Tomorrow is a 5-skill Content Language Integrated Learning (CLIL) textbook that focuses on technologies that will help us meet the 17 Sustainable Development Goals (SDGs) that were adopted by the United Nations in 2015. Although some high-level technical vocabulary is used, 70% of the words in the readings are inside the first 1000 most commonly used words of English. This allows L2 students to improve their language skills while at the same time learning the content.

The exercises and activities in this book are the result of empirical observation by the authors in their own classes, which makes this book attractive not only from the language point of view but also as a tool for teaching that has been proven to work.

This approach is very effective when used in conjunction with active learning strategies. Critical thinking is promoted in every unit through small group work and by questions that require students to find answers on their own.

1 Introduction

SUSTAINABLE DEVELOPMENT GOALS

At the end of this unit, you will ...

- ☐ understand what the SDGs are.
- ☐ understand why the SDGs were created.
- ☐ understand how working together helps the world.

Vocabulary Focus

A Match the words (1-12) with the correct definitions (a-l). The first one has been done for you!

1.	(b)	achievements	7.	( )	ensure
2.	( )	adopt	8.	( )	establish
3.	( )	advocacy	9.	( )	funding
4.	( )	combat	10.	( )	infrastructure
5.	( )	criticize	11.	( )	prosperity
6.	( )	empower	12.	( )	reduce

10 Our World Tomorrow

Every unit has a very appealing and easy to understand picture that gives an idea of what is going to be learned by the students.

Before starting a unit, the learning objectives are made clear, so students know what to expect.

Before starting, a Vocabulary Focus exercise challenges students on advanced vocabulary that is necessary in order to fully understand the main text.

About this book

B *Complete the sentences with the words from MATCHING. You may need to change the word form.*

1. The park was built with ______ from the city, so everyone can enjoy it for free.
2. When everyone has enough food and a happy home, our community is ______.
3. The roads, bridges, and tunnels make up the ______ of our city and help us get around.
4. We can help the planet by ______ the amount of trash we throw away.
5. When you learn how to ride a bike, it ______ you to go on adventures by yourself.

C *Write two original sentences using words from MATCHING to help you remember them.*

1.

2.

During the gap-fill activity, students must, once again, make sure they know all the additional unit vocabulary.

In addition, by having students create their own sentences, instructors can explain vocabulary with different meanings.

The main unit text, with 70% or more within the 1000 most common words of English, helps ensure that even students with lower levels of English proficiency can grasp the content. The work done in Vocabulary Focus helps ensure that additional vocabulary is covered before students engage with the unit text.

Additionally, notes in Japanese are available for specific technical vocabulary to help students fully engage with the text.

Reading

Read this passage carefully and underline any unknown words.

Working Together for a Better World

The Sustainable Development Goals (SDGs) are a set of global goals **adopted** by the United Nations in 2015 to end poverty, protect the planet, and ensure peace and **prosperity** for all people. There are 17 SDGs in total, and they cover a wide range of issues such as education, health, inequality, climate change, and clean energy.

Setting up goals for a better world is not something new. Just like the SDGs aim at **promoting** sustainable development by 2030, the Millennium Development Goals (MDGs) were a set of eight development goals **established** by the United Nations in 2000, with the aim of **reducing** poverty and **promoting** sustainable development by the year 2015. The goals included reducing *extreme poverty and hunger, achieving universal primary education, promoting gender equality and **empowering** women, reducing *child mortality, improving maternal health, **combating** HIV/AIDS, malaria, and other diseases, **ensuring** environmental sustainability, and developing a global partnership for development.

Although the MDGs were not fully achieved, significant progress was made in certain areas. According to the World Bank, in the year 2000, about 1.2 billion people were living in extreme poverty. This number went down to about 700 million in 2015 and it was one of the key **achievements** of the Millennium Development Goals (MDGs). Some of the reasons why the MDGs were not fully achieved include lack of **funding**, inadequate **infrastructure**, and not enough coordination. Additionally, the goals were **criticized** for being too broad and not specific enough, and for not considering the different needs and challenges faced by different countries and regions.

Setting up such goals is essential because it helps us think about how our actions today will affect people and the planet in the future. By focusing on long-term goals, we can ensure that our actions are sustainable and do not harm future generations. Achieving the SDGs will require collaboration and cooperation between governments, businesses, society, and individuals around the world. Everyone has a role to play in achieving these goals, whether it's through **advocacy**, volunteering, or making changes in our daily lives. Even if we cannot achieve 100% of all SDG goals, the most important thing is that we are all working together.

361 words: ___ minutes ___ seconds

Notes:
- extreme poverty the World Bank defines as less than $1.90 US per person per day
- child mortality 幼児死亡率

Because the MDGs were set in 2000 and the SDGs in 2015, it is likely that the global community will create a new set of goals after 2030.

12 Our World Tomorrow

Understanding

A *Choose the best answer(s) to each question.*

1. The SDGs were created to promote sustainable development by what year?
   a. 2000 b. 2015 c. 2030
2. What is one reason why the MDGs were not fully achieved?
   a. little coordination
   b. quality
   c. they were too broad
3. What is the most important part of the SDGs?
   a. There will be no poor people in the world.
   b. We all work together for a better world.
   c. We consider different countries and regions.

B *Answer the following questions. Use complete and grammatically correct sentences.*

1. What are the Sustainable Development Goals (SDGs)?
2. What was one of the key achievements of the Millennium Development Goals (MDGs)?
3. Why is it important to work towards meeting the SDG goals, even if they may not be fully achieved?

C *The following statements have mistakes. Correct them.*

1. The SDGs aim at ending wealth.
2. The MDGs aimed to achieve sustainable destruction by 2010.
3. The SDGs will be fully achieved by 2020.

1. Introduction 13

Comprehension of the text is crucial for students to understand the content of the unit. In this part, students are required to go back into the text and find answers. The comprehension section is conveniently placed on the opposite page so that students have access to the text.

To further test students' understanding, section C requires students to fix misleading statements. All the information, again, is available in the text on the left page.

Extra vocabulary work is done with synonyms by exploring words with meanings that are context dependent.

In the first section of Listening (A), the students listen to a spoken prompt (unwritten) and choose the best option. The second section (B), is a dictation task where the students write the missing phrases or sentences. All the audio files are available for download.

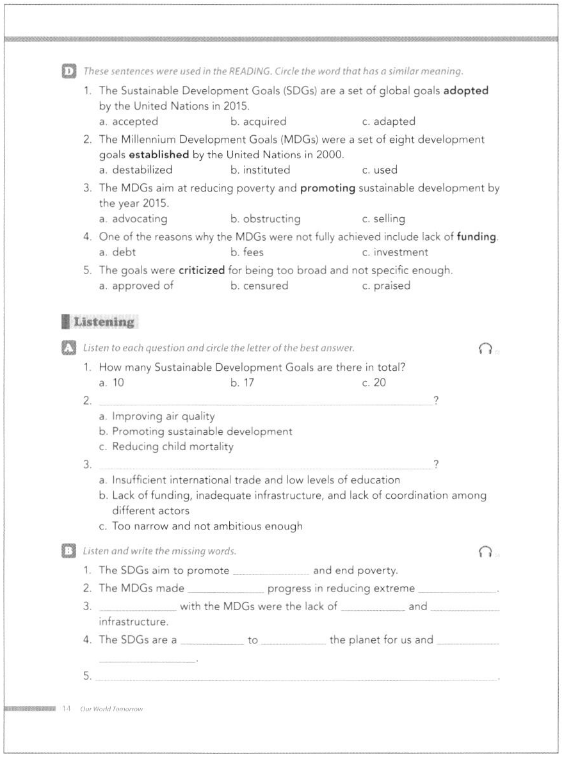
D *These sentences were used in the READING. Circle the word that has a similar meaning.*

1. The Sustainable Development Goals (SDGs) are a set of global goals **adopted** by the United Nations in 2015.
   a. accepted b. acquired c. adapted
2. The Millennium Development Goals (MDGs) were a set of eight development goals **established** by the United Nations in 2000.
   a. destabilized b. instituted c. used
3. The MDGs aim at reducing poverty and **promoting** sustainable development by the year 2015.
   a. advocating b. obstructing c. selling
4. One of the reasons why the MDGs were not fully achieved include lack of **funding**.
   a. debt b. fees c. investment
5. The goals were **criticized** for being too broad and not specific enough.
   a. approved of b. censured c. praised

Listening

A *Listen to each question and circle the letter of the best answer.*

1. How many Sustainable Development Goals are there in total?
   a. 10 b. 17 c. 20
2. ______________________________?
   a. Improving air quality
   b. Promoting sustainable development
   c. Reducing child mortality
3. ______________________________?
   a. Insufficient international trade and low levels of education
   b. Lack of funding, inadequate infrastructure, and lack of coordination among different actors
   c. Too narrow and not ambitious enough

B *Listen and write the missing words.*

1. The SDGs aim to promote ______ and end poverty.
2. The MDGs made ______ progress in reducing extreme ______.
3. ______ with the MDGs were the lack of ______ and ______ infrastructure.
4. The SDGs are a ______ to ______ the planet for us and ______.
5. ______________________________.

14 Our World Tomorrow

Discussion prompts can be used to facilitate pair or small group discussion. This helps the students to relate to the contents of the unit. These prompts promote knowledge sharing among students. Notes and drawings can be taken directly in the textbook.

Located in the Appendix, Sharing Information is a speaking and listening information-gap activity where students interact each other.

At the end of the unit, students can check their learning progress by checking which learning objectives have been met.

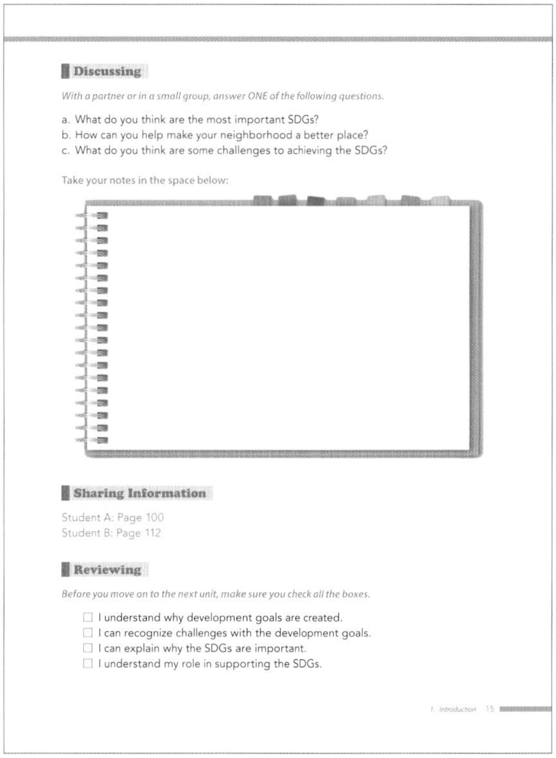
Discussing

With a partner or in a small group, answer ONE of the following questions.

a. What do you think are the most important SDGs?
b. How can you help make your neighborhood a better place?
c. What do you think are some challenges to achieving the SDGs?

Take your notes in the space below:

Sharing Information

Student A: Page 100
Student B: Page 112

Reviewing

Before you move on to the next unit, make sure you check all the boxes.

☐ I understand why development goals are created.
☐ I can recognize challenges with the development goals.
☐ I can explain why the SDGs are important.
☐ I understand my role in supporting the SDGs.

1 Introduction 15

About this book

Review units are presented to students to consolidate knowledge every four units. Questions similar in format to the TOEIC cover the following skills:

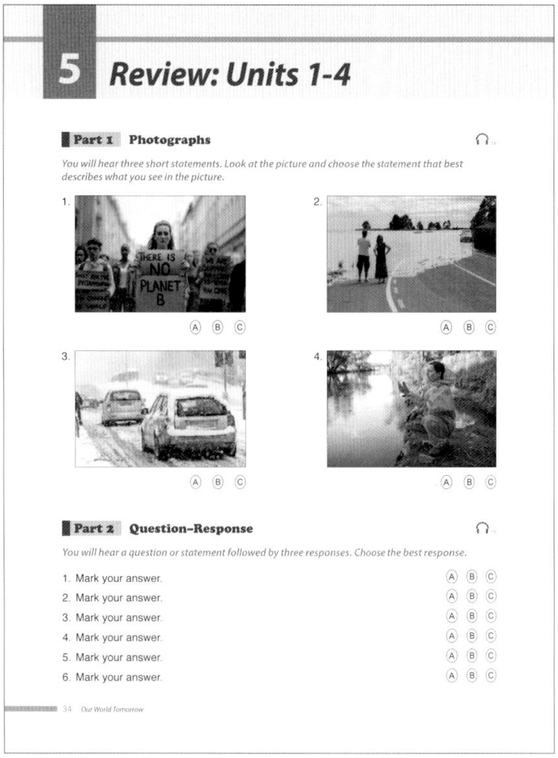

5 Review: Units 1-4

Part 1 **Photographs**

You will hear three short statements. Look at the picture and choose the statement that best describes what you see in the picture.

1\. Ⓐ Ⓑ Ⓒ

2\. Ⓐ Ⓑ Ⓒ

3\. Ⓐ Ⓑ Ⓒ

4\. Ⓐ Ⓑ Ⓒ

Part 2 **Question-Response**

You will hear a question or statement followed by three responses. Choose the best response.

1. Mark your answer. Ⓐ Ⓑ Ⓒ
2. Mark your answer. Ⓐ Ⓑ Ⓒ
3. Mark your answer. Ⓐ Ⓑ Ⓒ
4. Mark your answer. Ⓐ Ⓑ Ⓒ
5. Mark your answer. Ⓐ Ⓑ Ⓒ
6. Mark your answer. Ⓐ Ⓑ Ⓒ

34 Our World Tomorrow

Listening

- Photographs (4)
- Question-Response (6)
- Short Conversations (2)
- Short Talk (1)

Reading

- Text Completion (1)
- Reading Comprehension (1)

Integrated Skills

- Case Study (1)

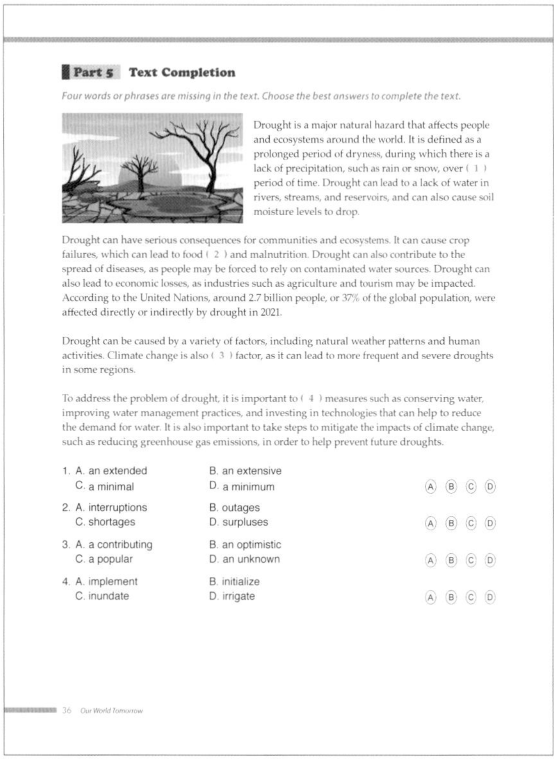

Part 5 **Text Completion**

Four words or phrases are missing in the text. Choose the best answers to complete the text.

Drought is a major natural hazard that affects people and ecosystems around the world. It is defined as a prolonged period of dryness, during which there is a lack of precipitation, such as rain or snow, over (1) period of time. Drought can lead to a lack of water in rivers, streams, and reservoirs, and can also cause soil moisture levels to drop.

Drought can have serious consequences for communities and ecosystems. It can cause crop failures, which can lead to food (2) and malnutrition. Drought can also contribute to the spread of diseases, as people may be forced to rely on contaminated water sources. Drought can also lead to economic losses, as industries such as agriculture and tourism may be impacted. According to the United Nations, around 2.7 billion people, or 37% of the global population, were affected directly or indirectly by drought in 2021.

Drought can be caused by a variety of factors, including natural weather patterns and human activities. Climate change is also (3) factor, as it can lead to more frequent and severe droughts in some regions.

To address the problem of drought, it is important to (4) measures such as conserving water, improving water management practices, and investing in technologies that can help to reduce the demand for water. It is also important to take steps to mitigate the impacts of climate change, such as reducing greenhouse gas emissions, in order to help prevent future droughts.

1. A. an extended B. an extensive C. a minimal D. a minimum Ⓐ Ⓑ Ⓒ Ⓓ
2. A. interruptions B. outages C. shortages D. surpluses Ⓐ Ⓑ Ⓒ Ⓓ
3. A. a contributing B. an optimistic C. a popular D. an unknown Ⓐ Ⓑ Ⓒ Ⓓ
4. A. implement B. initialize C. inundate D. irrigate Ⓐ Ⓑ Ⓒ Ⓓ

36 Our World Tomorrow

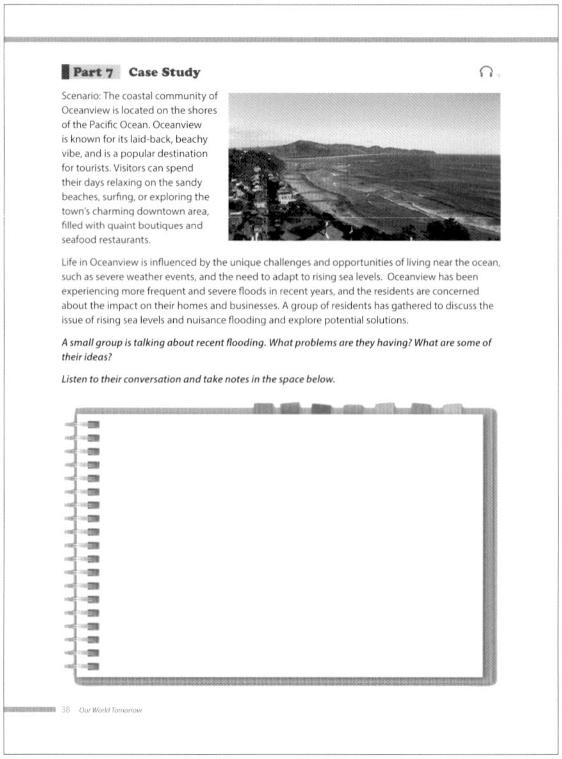

Part 7 **Case Study**

Scenario: The coastal community of Oceanview is located on the shores of the Pacific Ocean. Oceanview is known for its laid-back, beachy vibe, and is a popular destination for tourists. Visitors can spend their days relaxing on the sandy beaches, surfing, or exploring the town's charming downtown area, filled with quaint boutiques and seafood restaurants.

Life in Oceanview is influenced by the unique challenges and opportunities of living near the ocean, such as severe weather events, and the need to adapt to rising sea levels. Oceanview has been experiencing more frequent and severe floods in recent years, and the residents are concerned about the impact on their homes and businesses. A group of residents has gathered to discuss the issue of rising sea levels and nuisance flooding and explore potential solutions.

A small group is talking about recent flooding. What problems are they having? What are some of their ideas?

Listen to their conversation and take notes in the space below.

38 Our World Tomorrow

If you have students who are hungry for even more knowledge, Information Sharing activities are available in the Appendix. Pair Reading and information-gap charts extend the usability of the book even more, making it a great tool to promote speaking and listening.

These activities can also be used to introduce target language that instructors want to cover.

For instructors wishing to extend their lessons, additional photocopiable materials are available in the Teacher's Manual, including Single and Pair Crosswords as well as sample lesson plans and unit tests.

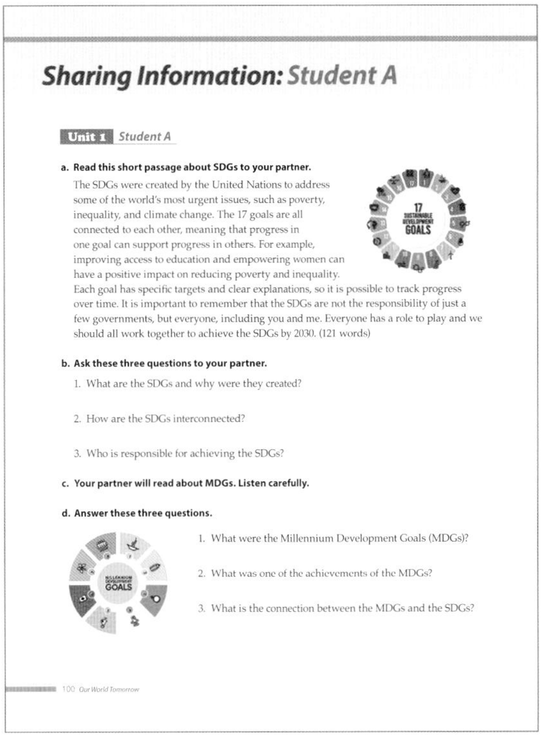

Sharing Information: Student A

Unit 1 *Student A*

a. Read this short passage about SDGs to your partner.

The SDGs were created by the United Nations to address some of the world's most urgent issues, such as poverty, inequality, and climate change. The 17 goals are all connected to each other, meaning that progress in one goal can support progress in others. For example, improving access to education and empowering women can have a positive impact on reducing poverty and inequality. Each goal has specific targets and clear explanations, so it is possible to track progress over time. It is important to remember that the SDGs are not the responsibility of just a few governments, but everyone, including you and me. Everyone has a role to play and we should all work together to achieve the SDGs by 2030. (121 words)

b. Ask these three questions to your partner.

1. What are the SDGs and why were they created?
2. How are the SDGs interconnected?
3. Who is responsible for achieving the SDGs?

c. Your partner will read about MDGs. Listen carefully.

d. Answer these three questions.

1. What were the Millennium Development Goals (MDGs)?
2. What was one of the achievements of the MDGs?
3. What is the connection between the MDGs and the SDGs?

100 *Our World Tomorrow*

We would like to thank you for choosing *Our World Tomorrow* and we hope the content and activities will help you teach your course successfully. Class activities and homework tasks can and should go beyond the scope of this book, but we really hope this textbook to be an easy to understand and use educational tool for both instructors and students.

Adam and Anderson

Contents

1 Introduction

At the end of this unit, you will …

- ☐ understand what the SDGs are.
- ☐ understand why the SDGs were created.
- ☐ understand how working together helps the world.

Vocabulary Focus

A *Match the words (1-12) with the correct definitions (a-l). The first one has been done for you!*

1.	(b)	achievements	7.	( )	ensure
2.	( )	adopt	8.	( )	establish
3.	( )	advocacy	9.	( )	funding
4.	( )	combat	10.	( )	infrastructure
5.	( )	criticize	11.	( )	prosperity
6.	( )	empower	12.	( )	reduce

a. supporting something publicly
b. something you have accomplished or done well
c. when things are going well and people are successful and happy
d. to make sure that something will happen or be done
e. money that is given to support a project or an organization
f. to fight against something or someone
g. the basic facilities, systems, and structures needed by a community to function properly
h. to start something and make it officially recognized
i. to start doing or using something
j. to say something negative about something or someone
k. make something smaller or less in amount
l. to give someone the ability and power to do something

B *Complete the sentences with the words from MATCHING. You may need to change the word form.*

1. The park was built with ________________ from the city, so everyone can enjoy it for free.
2. When everyone has enough food and a happy home, our community is ________________.
3. The roads, bridges, and tunnels make up the ________________ of our city and help us get around.
4. We can help the planet by ________________ the amount of trash we throw away.
5. When you learn how to ride a bike, it ________________ you to go on adventures by yourself.

C *Write two original sentences using words from MATCHING to help you remember them.*

1.
2.

Reading

02

Read this passage carefully and underline any unknown words.

Working Together for a Better World

The Sustainable Development Goals (SDGs) are a set of global goals **adopted** by the United Nations in 2015 to end poverty, protect the planet, and ensure peace and **prosperity** for all people. There are 17 SDGs in total, and they cover a wide range of issues such as education, health, inequality, climate change, and clean energy.

Setting up goals for a better world is not something new. Just like the SDGs aim at **promoting** sustainable development by 2030, the Millennium Development Goals (MDGs) were a set of eight development goals **established** by the United Nations in 2000, with the aim of **reducing** poverty and **promoting** sustainable development by the year 2015. The goals included reducing *extreme poverty and hunger, achieving universal primary education, promoting gender equality and **empowering** women, reducing *child mortality, improving maternal health, **combating** HIV/AIDS, malaria, and other diseases, **ensuring** environmental sustainability, and developing a global partnership for development.

Although the MDGs were not fully achieved, significant progress was made in certain areas. According to the World Bank, in the year 2000, about 1.2 billion people were living in extreme poverty. This number went down to about 700 million in 2015 and it was one of the key **achievements** of the Millennium Development Goals (MDGs). Some of the reasons why the MDGs were not fully achieved include lack of **funding**, inadequate **infrastructure**, and not enough coordination. Additionally, the goals were **criticized** for being too broad and not specific enough, and for not considering the different needs and challenges faced by different countries and regions.

Setting up such goals is essential because it helps us think about how our actions today will affect people and the planet in the future. By focusing on long-term goals, we can ensure that our actions are sustainable and do not harm future generations. Achieving the SDGs will require collaboration and cooperation between governments, businesses, society, and individuals around the world. Everyone has a role to play in achieving these goals, whether it's through **advocacy**, volunteering, or making changes in our daily lives. Even if we cannot achieve 100% of all SDG goals, the most important thing is that we are all working together.

361 words: ____ minutes ____ seconds

Notes:

- extreme poverty　the World Bank defines as less than $1.90 US per person per day
- child mortality　幼児死亡率

Because the MDGs were set in 2000 and the SDGs in 2015, it is likely that the global community will create a new set of goals after 2030.

Understanding

A *Choose the best answer(s) to each question.*

1. The SDGs were created to promote sustainable development by what year?
   a. 2000 b. 2015 c. 2030
2. What is one reason why the MDGs were not fully achieved?
   a. little coordination
   b. quality
   c. they were too broad
3. What is the most important part of the SDGs?
   a. There will be no poor people in the world.
   b. We all work together for a better world.
   c. We consider different countries and regions.

B *Answer the following questions. Use complete and grammatically correct sentences.*

1. What are the Sustainable Development Goals (SDGs)?
2. What was one of the key achievements of the Millennium Development Goals (MDGs)?
3. Why is it important to work towards meeting the SDG goals, even if they may not be fully achieved?

C *The following statements have mistakes. Correct them.*

1. The SDGs aim at ending wealth.
2. The MDGs aimed to achieve sustainable destruction by 2010.
3. The SDGs will be fully achieved by 2020.

D *These sentences were used in the READING. Circle the word that has a similar meaning.*

1. The Sustainable Development Goals (SDGs) are a set of global goals **adopted** by the United Nations in 2015.
   a. accepted　　b. acquired　　c. adapted
2. The Millennium Development Goals (MDGs) were a set of eight development goals **established** by the United Nations in 2000.
   a. destabilized　　b. instituted　　c. used
3. The MDGs aim at reducing poverty and **promoting** sustainable development by the year 2015.
   a. advocating　　b. obstructing　　c. selling
4. One of the reasons why the MDGs were not fully achieved include lack of **funding**.
   a. debt　　b. fees　　c. investment
5. The goals were **criticized** for being too broad and not specific enough.
   a. approved of　　b. censured　　c. praised

Listening

A *Listen to each question and circle the letter of the best answer.* 03

1. How many Sustainable Development Goals are there in total?
   a. 10　　b. 17　　c. 20
2. ____?
   a. Improving air quality
   b. Promoting sustainable development
   c. Reducing child mortality
3. ____?
   a. Insufficient international trade and low levels of education
   b. Lack of funding, inadequate infrastructure, and lack of coordination among different actors
   c. Too narrow and not ambitious enough

B *Listen and write the missing words.* 04

1. The SDGs aim to promote ____________ and end poverty.
2. The MDGs made ____________ progress in reducing extreme ____________.
3. ____________ with the MDGs were the lack of ____________ and ____________ infrastructure.
4. The SDGs are a ____________ to ____________ the planet for us and ____________ ____________.
5. ____.

Discussing

With a partner or in a small group, answer ONE of the following questions.

a. What do you think are the most important SDGs?
b. How can you help make your neighborhood a better place?
c. What do you think are some challenges to achieving the SDGs?

Take your notes in the space below:

Sharing Information

Student A: Page 100
Student B: Page 112

Reviewing

Before you move on to the next unit, make sure you check all the boxes.

- ☐ I understand why development goals are created.
- ☐ I can recognize challenges with the development goals.
- ☐ I can explain why the SDGs are important.
- ☐ I understand my role in supporting the SDGs.

2 Good Health

At the end of this unit, you will ...

- ☐ understand different types of health-tracking devices.
- ☐ understand the kinds of data collected by health-tracking devices.
- ☐ understand what e-coaching is.

Vocabulary Focus

A *Match the words (1-12) with the correct definitions (a-l). The first one has been done for you!*

1.	(g)	behavior	7.	(　)	epidemic
2.	(　)	chronic	8.	(　)	gadget
3.	(　)	correlated	9.	(　)	glimpse
4.	(　)	crowdsource	10.	(　)	monitor
5.	(　)	diagnose	11.	(　)	pervasive
6.	(　)	dose	12.	(　)	wearable

a. things that are closely connected and affect or depend on each other
b. a small mechanical or electronic device that does something useful
c. to identify an illness or the cause of a problem
d. to see for a short time or a small part of something
e. a large number of cases of a disease at the same time
f. to get information or help from a large number of people, by using the internet
g. the way someone acts or does to make something happen
h. a device that can be worn and often includes tracking information related to health and fitness
i. lasting for a long time; difficult to cure
j. to watch and check something over time
k. throughout every part of something
l. the amount of a medicine taken at one time

B *Complete the sentences with the words from MATCHING. You may need to change the word form.*

1. Because of advances in electronics, the number of ____________ has greatly increased.
2. To improve your health, you need to change your eating ____________.
3. The new professional sports team ____________ names for their new mascot.
4. The man became quite sick when he took the wrong ____________ of the medication.
5. The retired athlete suffered from ____________ back pain.

C *Write two original sentences using words from MATCHING to help you remember them.*

1.
2.

Reading

05

Read this passage carefully and underline any unknown words.

Technology Empowers Users to Keep Their Well-being

In recent years, **wearables** such as smartphones and fitness trackers have become increasingly popular tools for **pervasive** health **monitoring**. Devices such as smartwatches gather general information while *glucose level detectors collect specific data. People have a seemingly endless number of devices to choose from, not only for gathering data about themselves, but also ways to share their data with a variety of applications and professional institutions. This data can be used to create general health or fitness reports or even personalized coaching-style advice and recommendations.

Simple things like tracking how many steps you walk in a day or tracking your heartbeat provide us with a **glimpse** of how personal these **gadgets** can be. Data can be retrieved not only from the sensors in wearables, but also from sensors in our homes and workplaces. For example, **monitoring** temperature and air quality has become an important feature for people who suffer from **chronic** respiratory problems. Not only is data collected, but changes in a user's everyday behavior can be detected and be **correlated** with health events to understand one's health better. One of the biggest advantages of these devices is that data can be used in real-time to help people with known health conditions monitor their everyday activities. Also, in extreme cases, these devices can contact health services where doctors can **monitor** daily **doses** of medication.

E-coaching is a promising use of the data collected. Like a human coach, an intelligent computer system observes and then analyzes the user's data to make predictions and give specific advice to help them reach their health or fitness-related goal. For many people, e-coaching helps create and maintain healthy behaviors related to nutrition and exercise.

These are just some examples of how technology can help individuals maintain their well-being. Wearable devices produce a great amount of data that can help **diagnose** health problems and provide individualized coaching. Finally, using **crowdsourced** data can help improve everyone's quality of life, since the large-scale **monitoring** and analysis of data may help us better understand current illnesses and identify new **epidemics**.

341 words: ____ minutes ____ seconds

Notes:

- glucose グルコース

Understanding

A *Choose the best answer(s) to each question.*

1. What kind of data do smartwatches gather?
   a. all　　b. general　　c. specific
2. What information about the air is important for people with respiratory problems?
   a. humidity　　b. quality　　c. temperature
3. How can wearable devices help us better understand current illnesses?
   a. By diagnosing health problems
   b. By providing individualized coaching
   c. By sharing data so it can be crowdsourced

B *Answer the following questions. Use complete and grammatically correct sentences.*

1. What are some examples of data collected by wearables?

   ....

   ....

2. What is e-coaching? How does it work?

   ....

   ....

3. How can crowdsourced data be used?

   ....

   ....

C *The following statements have mistakes. Correct them.*

1. A person's glucose level is general information.

   ....

2. A user's behavior is unrelated to health events.

   ....

3. Wearable devices generate a limited amount of data.

   ....

D *These sentences were used in the READING. Circle the word that has a similar meaning.*

1. Users have a seemingly **endless** number of devices to choose from.
   a. countless b. few c. many
2. They provide us with a **glimpse** of how personal these gadgets can be.
   a. awareness b. confusion c. misunderstanding
3. The data can be used in real-time to help people with **known** health conditions.
   a. acknowledged b. important c. secret
4. Data may help us better understand current illnesses and identify new **epidemics**.
   a. explosions b. outbreaks c. waves
5. E-coaching can help create and **maintain** healthy behaviors.
   a. abandon b. eliminate c. keep

Listening

A *Listen to each question and circle the letter of the best answer.* 06

1. What does a wearable do with the data gathered from a user?
   a. it checks glucose level
   b. it gives recommendations
   c. it monitors the air quality
2. ____?
   a. they can expose behavior changes
   b. they control the temperature
   c. they help understand our health
3. ____?
   a. altitude
   b. heartbeat
   c. weather forecast

B *Listen and write the missing words.* 07

1. Since I bought ____________________, I have been drinking more water each day.
2. Mr. Draper had an ____________________ detected by his smartwatch.
3. I need __________ steps ____________ my target.
4. I am ____________________ my ____________ for ______________.
5. ____.

Discussing

With a partner or in a small group, answer ONE of the following questions.

a. What wearables are popular in your country? Do you have one?
b. What health or fitness-related goal do you have?
c. What do you think about e-coaching?

Take your notes in the space below:

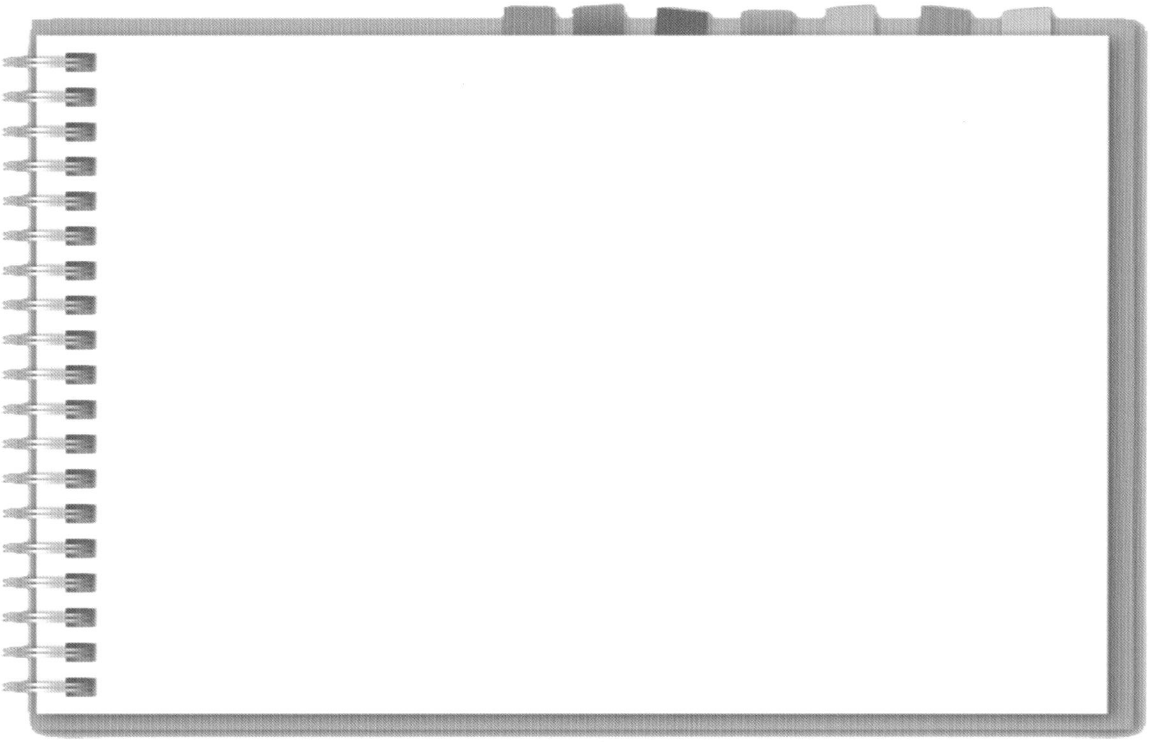

Sharing Information

Student A: Page 101
Student B: Page 113

Reviewing

Before you move on to the next unit, make sure you check all the boxes.

- ☐ I can describe the different types of health-tracking devices.
- ☐ I can give some examples of the data collected by health-tracking devices.
- ☐ I can explain e-coaching.
- ☐ I can list some possible uses for crowdsourced data.

3 Breaking the Poverty Cycle

At the end of this unit, you will ...

☐ understand how the poverty cycle works.
☐ understand the impacts of the poverty cycle on communities.
☐ understand some ways to break the poverty cycle.

Vocabulary Focus

A *Match the words (1-12) with the correct definitions (a-l). The first one has been done for you!*

1.	(j)	crucial	7.	( )	mechanism
2.	( )	debt	8.	( )	perpetuate
3.	( )	degrading	9.	( )	phenomenon
4.	( )	equitable	10.	( )	root
5.	( )	ethnicity	11.	( )	systemic
6.	( )	insurance	12.	( )	trap

a. the way something works or happens
b. the cause or source of something
c. a promise to help pay for things if something goes wrong
d. something that happens or exists that is noticeable and interesting
e. to continue something so that it doesn't stop
f. something that is connected to a whole system or group, rather than just one part
g. to make something worse, especially if it is something that is already not good
h. fair and just, so that everyone is treated equally
i. where someone's family comes from and what their cultural traditions are
j. very important or necessary
k. to get stuck in something that is hard to get out of
l. owing someone money

B *Complete the sentences with the words from MATCHING. You may need to change the word form.*

1. It is ________________ to drink water every day to stay healthy.
2. Bullying ________________ a cycle of hurt and sadness.
3. Climate change is a(n) ________________ issue that affects the whole planet.
4. We must ensure that everyone has a(n) ________________ chance to succeed in life.
5. My car ________________ helps pay for repairs if I get into an accident.

C *Write two original sentences using words from MATCHING to help you remember them.*

1.
2.

Reading

08

Read this passage carefully and underline any unknown words.

The Poverty Cycle

Poverty is a very complex issue that is usually linked with factors such as unemployment, low wages, lack of access to education and healthcare, and discrimination. The poverty cycle is a **phenomenon** where individuals or families become **trapped** in a cycle of poverty that is difficult to break. It is a self-reinforcing **mechanism** that **perpetuates** poverty across generations.

The poverty cycle has a significant impact on the economical development of a country. As poverty leads to poor health and nutrition, it reduces people's productivity. Also, with limited resources to invest into basic areas like education and infrastructure, poverty also limits opportunities for job creation and entrepreneurship. Governments may need to spend more on social protection programs, such as food *subsidies, healthcare, and education, to support those living in poverty. This can increase government **debt** and reduce resources available for investment in other areas. A lack of investment in education and infrastructure can limit a country's competitiveness in the global marketplace. This can reduce opportunities for trade and foreign investment which limits economic growth. As we can see, the effects of poverty are very negative and addressing poverty is essential not just for moral reasons but also for sustainable economic development.

To break this cycle, it is important to create job opportunities, provide social protection and access to *basic services, promote economic growth and sustainable development, and address **systemic** inequalities. Job creation is **crucial** to reduce poverty. Governments and businesses can invest in job creation programs, such as *vocational training, *entrepreneurship development, and public works projects. Social protection programs, such as cash transfers, food subsidies, and health **insurance**, can help to provide a basic safety net for the poorest and most vulnerable populations. Economic growth can create more opportunities for jobs, investment, and entrepreneurship, leading to greater *prosperity for all. Governments can promote policies that support economic growth, such as infrastructure development and investment in key sectors, of course, without **degrading** the natural environment. Poverty is often **rooted** in **systemic** inequalities, such as discrimination based on gender, race, **ethnicity**, or socioeconomic status. Addressing these inequalities is **crucial** to reducing poverty and creating a more just and **equitable** society.

355 words: ____ minutes ____ seconds

Notes:
- subsidies 補助金 • basic service ベーシックサービス（生きるための医療、教育、障害福祉などの最低限の保障のこと） • vocational training 職業訓練 • entrepreneurship 起業家精神 • prosperity 繁栄

Understanding

A *Choose the best answer(s) to each question.*

1. Which of the following is NOT a factor linked to poverty?
   a. discrimination   b. high wages   c. unemployment
2. How does poverty impact a country's economic development?
   a. It decreases government debt.
   b. It increases investment opportunities.
   c. It limits opportunities for job creation and entrepreneurship.
3. Which of the following is an important strategy for breaking the poverty cycle?
   a. Decreasing investment in infrastructure development
   b. Discriminating against certain groups
   c. Promoting economic growth and sustainable development

B *Answer the following questions. Use complete and grammatically correct sentences.*

1. What are some factors that are linked to poverty, and how do they contribute to the poverty cycle?
2. What are some of the negative impacts of poverty on individuals, communities, and countries, and why is it important to address poverty for sustainable economic development?
3. What are some examples of social protection programs that can help to support those living in poverty?

C *The following statements have mistakes. Correct them.*

1. Poverty is only caused by lack of access to education and healthcare.
2. Governments should invest less in social protection programs to avoid increasing their debt.
3. Creating job opportunities is the only solution to breaking the poverty cycle.

D *These sentences were used in the READING. Circle the word that has a similar meaning.*

1. It is a **self-reinforcing** mechanism.
   a. self-defeating　　b. self-destructive　　c. self-perpetuating
2. The poverty cycle has a **significant** impact on economic development.
   a. meaningful　　b. minor　　c. trivial
3. A **lack** of investment in education and infrastructure can limit a country's competitiveness.
   a. abundance　　b. raise　　c. shortage
4. Governments can **promote** policies that support economic growth.
   a. obstruct　　b. prompt　　c. support

Listening

A *Listen to each question and circle the letter of the best answer.* 09

1. What are some factors usually linked with poverty?
   a. Employment and education
   b. Healthcare and discrimination
   c. Unemployment and lack of access to education and healthcare
2. ______________________________?
   a. A process that breaks the cycle of poverty
   b. A self-reinforcing mechanism that perpetuates poverty across generations
   c. A strategy to address systemic inequalities
3. ______________________________?
   a. Creating job opportunities and provide social protection
   b. Increasing systemic inequalities
   c. Limiting investment in education and infrastructure

B *Listen and write the missing words.* 10

1. Climate change is a __________ that is affecting the entire planet.
2. Human activities are __________ the natural environment at an __________ rate.
3. To promote __________, it is important to address __________.
4. Discrimination __________ is a serious __________ around the world.
5. ______________________________.

Discussing

With a partner or in a small group, answer ONE of the following questions.

a. How does poverty affect people?
b. What are some things that can be done to help break the poverty cycle?
c. How can we help people who are living in poverty in our community?

Take your notes in the space below:

Sharing Information

Student A: Page 102
Student B: Page 114

Reviewing

Before you move on to the next unit, make sure you check all the boxes.

☐ I understand how the poverty cycle works.
☐ I understand the impacts of the poverty cycle on communities.
☐ I understand ways to break the poverty cycle.

4 Clean Water

At the end of this unit, you will …

- ☐ understand how parts of the world manage water supplies.
- ☐ understand some processes for treating water.
- ☐ understand technical vocabulary related to water.

Vocabulary Focus

A *Match the words (1-12) with the correct definitions (a-l). The first one has been done for you!*

1.	(c)	bacteria	7.	( )	impurity
2.	( )	condense	8.	( )	irrigation
3.	( )	contaminate	9.	( )	membrane
4.	( )	desalination	10.	( )	permeable
5.	( )	distill	11.	( )	pollutant
6.	( )	hygiene	12.	( )	thermal

a. the habit of keeping clean to prevent sickness and disease
b. a thin layer of material that makes a barrier or lining
c. the simplest and smallest form of life
d. something that makes air, water, etc. unpleasant or dangerous to use
e. to make a pure liquid by making it gas, then cooling it and collecting the drops of liquid
f. a substance that makes something dirty or lower quality
g. the process of supplying water to farmland
h. to make something unusable by making it impure or unclean
i. allows liquid or gas to pass through
j. to change a gas into a liquid
k. related to heat
l. the process of removing salt from water, usually seawater

B *Complete the sentences with the words from MATCHING. You may need to change the word form.*

1. Brushing your teeth every day is an essential part of oral ________________.
2. Industrial processes can ________________ the air and soil with harmful chemicals.
3. Regular cleaning of air conditioners helps prevent the growth of mold and ________________.
4. The presence of ________________ in the metal reduced its overall strength and quality.
5. ________________ water is often used in steam irons because it does not leave mineral deposits on clothes.

C *Write two original sentences.*

1.
2.

Reading

11

Read this passage carefully and underline any unknown words.

Desalination

Clean water is water that is safe to drink, use for cooking, and use for personal **hygiene**. It is free from **contaminants** that could cause illness or harm. Access to clean water is essential for human health.

It is important to regularly test water to ensure that it is clean and safe to drink. It should be tested for a range of **contaminants**, including **bacteria**, viruses, and chemical pollutants. If the water is found to be **contaminated**, it will likely need to be treated. One common method is to treat water with chemicals such as *chlorine to kill harmful bacteria and viruses. Water can also be treated by passing it through a series of filters to remove **impurities** and **contaminants**. In some cases, a combination of methods is used to ensure that it is drinkable.

In many parts of the world, there is a shortage of fresh water, or the available water is low quality. **Desalination** is widely used as a way to provide water. **Desalination** plants, like the one in the photograph, are used around the world to produce fresh water for 300 million people, and for **irrigation** and other agricultural purposes. **Desalination** is the process of removing salt and other minerals from *brackish water or seawater, making it drinkable. Typically, the seawater is forced through a **membrane** that separates the salt and other minerals from the water. There are several different methods of **desalination** such as *reverse osmosis, *electrodialysis, and thermal **distillation**.

Reverse osmosis is the most common method used by **desalination** plants. It works by forcing seawater through a **semipermeable membrane** under high pressure. The **membrane** allows water to pass through, but blocks salt and other minerals. The process requires a lot of energy along with chemicals and filters, but it is effective at producing high-quality drinking water.

Electrodialysis works by passing seawater through a series of **membranes** that are charged with electricity. The electricity causes the ions in the seawater (such as *sodium and *chloride) to move toward opposite electrodes, while the water molecules pass through the **membrane**. This process is less energy-intensive than reverse osmosis, but it is not as effective.

Thermal **distillation** works by heating seawater to the point where it turns into steam. The steam is then cooled and **condensed**, producing fresh water. This process is the most energy-intensive, but produces high-quality drinking water.

391 words: ____ minutes ____ seconds

Notes:

- chlorine 塩素系
- brackish 汽水
- reverse osmosis 逆浸透
- electrodialysis 電気透析
- sodium ナトリウム
- chloride 塩化物

Understanding

A *Choose the best answer(s) to each question.*

1. How can contaminated water be made drinkable?
   a. By adding a range of bacteria
   b. By running it through filters
   c. By treating it with chemicals

2. What is the main purpose of desalination?
   a. To convert seawater into fresh water
   b. To produce low-cost energy to coastal cities
   c. To remove impurities from contaminated water

3. Which desalination process uses steam?
   a. electrodialysis
   b. reverse osmosis
   c. thermal distillation

B *Answer the following questions. Use complete and grammatically correct sentences.*

1. What should drinking water be tested for?

2. Explain the process of desalination.

3. What is a major difference between reverse osmosis and electrodialysis?

C *The following statements have mistakes. Correct them.*

1. Electrodialysis is more energy efficient than reverse osmosis.

2. Reverse osmosis is the least widely used method of desalination.

3. Desalination plants are mainly used for agricultural purposes.

D *These sentences were used in the READING. Circle the word that has a similar meaning.*

1. Access to clean water is **essential** for human health.
   a. crucial   b. optional   c. voluntary
2. **Typically**, seawater is forced through a membrane that separates the salt.
   a. generally   b. rarely   c. seldom
3. The membrane **blocks** salt and other minerals.
   a. assists   b. impedes   c. permits
4. It should be tested for a **range** of contaminants.
   a. couple   b. few   c. variety

Listening

A *Listen to each question and circle the letter of the best answer.* 12

1. Which is the most common method of desalination?
   a. electrodialysis
   b. reverse osmosis
   c. thermal distillation
2. ____?
   a. brackish water
   b. freshwater
   c. seawater
3. ____?
   a. chloride
   b. chlorine
   c. sodium

B *Listen and write the missing words.* 13

1. Many cities treat their ______________ with chemicals such as chlorine.
2. Desalination plants are used to ______________________ from seawater.
3. A large stable supply of ________ is needed for ______________________.
4. ______ water is ________ for certain uses such as _______ and drinking.
5. ____
   ________________.

Discussing

With a partner or in a small group, answer ONE of the following questions.

a. How much water do you drink each day?
b. What would be the biggest impact in your life if there was a water shortage?
c. How can we reduce water use in our daily lives?

Take your notes in the space below:

Sharing Information

Student A: Page 103
Student B: Page 115

Reviewing

Before you move on to the next unit, make sure you check all the boxes.

- ☐ I can explain some methods of desalination.
- ☐ I can explain the different types of water.
- ☐ I can list some ways we can reduce water usage.

5 Review: Units 1-4

Part 1 Photographs

14

You will hear three short statements. Look at the picture and choose the statement that best describes what you see in the picture.

1\.

Ⓐ Ⓑ Ⓒ

2\.

Ⓐ Ⓑ Ⓒ

3\.

Ⓐ Ⓑ Ⓒ

4\.

Ⓐ Ⓑ Ⓒ

Part 2 Question-Response

15

You will hear a question or statement followed by three responses. Choose the best response.

1. Mark your answer. Ⓐ Ⓑ Ⓒ
2. Mark your answer. Ⓐ Ⓑ Ⓒ
3. Mark your answer. Ⓐ Ⓑ Ⓒ
4. Mark your answer. Ⓐ Ⓑ Ⓒ
5. Mark your answer. Ⓐ Ⓑ Ⓒ
6. Mark your answer. Ⓐ Ⓑ Ⓒ

Part 3 Short Conversations

16

You will hear short conversations between two people. Choose the best answer to each of the three questions.

Dialogue 1

1. Who are the speakers?
   A. A couple   B. Classmates
   C. Colleagues
   Ⓐ Ⓑ Ⓒ

2. What is the woman trying to organize?
   A. A course   B. A party
   C. A trip
   Ⓐ Ⓑ Ⓒ

3. What is the woman likely to do next?
   A. Give up on her plans   B. Go ahead with her plans
   C. Postpone her plans
   Ⓐ Ⓑ Ⓒ

Dialogue 2

1. Who are the speakers?
   A. Colleagues   B. Friends
   C. Strangers
   Ⓐ Ⓑ Ⓒ

2. What are they talking about?
   A. Becoming a coach   B. Finding a coach
   C. Getting more experience
   Ⓐ Ⓑ Ⓒ

3. What is the woman likely to do next?
   A. Get more information.   B. Make the decision.
   C. Rethink the plan.
   Ⓐ Ⓑ Ⓒ

Part 4 Short Talk

17

You will hear a short talk. Choose the best answer to each of the three questions.

1. Who is likely the speaker?
   A. An entrepreneur   B. A sales person
   C. A scientist   D. A reporter
   Ⓐ Ⓑ Ⓒ Ⓓ

2. Which places are most at risk?
   A. Coastal communities   B. Rural communities
   C. Metropolitan communities   D. Suburban communities
   Ⓐ Ⓑ Ⓒ Ⓓ

3. What solutions are mentioned?
   A. Adopting cleaner energy   B. Conserving energy
   C. Building new cities   D. Restoring structures
   Ⓐ Ⓑ Ⓒ Ⓓ

Part 5 Text Completion

Four words or phrases are missing in the text. Choose the best answers to complete the text.

Drought is a major natural hazard that affects people and ecosystems around the world. It is defined as a prolonged period of dryness, during which there is a lack of precipitation, such as rain or snow, over (1) period of time. Drought can lead to a lack of water in rivers, streams, and reservoirs, and can also cause soil moisture levels to drop.

Drought can have serious consequences for communities and ecosystems. It can cause crop failures, which can lead to food (2) and malnutrition. Drought can also contribute to the spread of diseases, as people may be forced to rely on contaminated water sources. Drought can also lead to economic losses, as industries such as agriculture and tourism may be impacted. According to the United Nations, around 2.7 billion people, or 37% of the global population, were affected directly or indirectly by drought in 2021.

Drought can be caused by a variety of factors, including natural weather patterns and human activities. Climate change is also (3) factor, as it can lead to more frequent and severe droughts in some regions.

To address the problem of drought, it is important to (4) measures such as conserving water, improving water management practices, and investing in technologies that can help to reduce the demand for water. It is also important to take steps to mitigate the impacts of climate change, such as reducing greenhouse gas emissions, in order to help prevent future droughts.

1. A. an extended B. an extensive
   C. a minimal D. a minimum (A) (B) (C) (D)

2. A. interruptions B. outages
   C. shortages D. surpluses (A) (B) (C) (D)

3. A. a contributing B. an optimistic
   C. a popular D. an unknown (A) (B) (C) (D)

4. A. implement B. initialize
   C. inundate D. irrigate (A) (B) (C) (D)

Part 6 Reading Comprehension

Read the following text. Choose the best answer to each question.

Attention all students and faculty!

Join us for a weekend lecture series on desertification and droughts, pressing global issues that affect millions of people around the world. Desertification is a process by which fertile land becomes degraded and turns into desert, often as a result of human activities such as overgrazing, deforestation, and improper irrigation. This process can have serious consequences for people and ecosystems.

WORLD DAY TO COMBAT
DESERTIFICATION AND DROUGHT
17 JUNE

Our lineup of expert speakers will explore the causes and consequences of desertification and drought, as well as current efforts to combat and reverse it.

June 17 (Saturday) - The Memorial Auditorium

10:00 am - 10:45 am	Introduction and opening remarks by Dr. J. Umbridge
11:00 am - 12:00 am	Lecture 1 - "The Science of Climate Change" by Dr. S. Coulson
12:30 pm - 2:00 pm	Lecture 2 - "The Link Between Climate Change and Drought" by Dr. R. Geller

June 18 (Sunday) - The Performing Arts Center

10:00 am - 10:30 am	Introduction and opening remarks by Dr. M. McGonagall
10:45 am - 11:45 am	Lecture 3 - "The Economic and Social Impact of Desertification and Drought" by Dr. W. White
1:00 pm - 2:30 pm	Lecture 4 - "The Future of Desertification and Drought: Predictions and Solutions" by Dr. P. Venkman

Admission is free, so bring your friends and family and come ready to learn about these critical issues. Please note that seating is limited, so we strongly encourage you registering to secure your spot. For inquiries, please call 903-268-TALK (8255).

1. Where is this text likely to be found?
   A. A business magazine B. A school newspaper
   C. An encyclopedia
   Ⓐ Ⓑ Ⓒ

2. Who is this event intended for?
   A. Children and teenagers B. The general public
   C. Scientists and experts
   Ⓐ Ⓑ Ⓒ

3. What is true about both days?
   A. The program ends at the same time each day.
   B. There are 15 minute breaks between sessions.
   C. There are 90 minute lectures on both days.
   Ⓐ Ⓑ Ⓒ

4. What should interested people do?
   A. Buy tickets in advance B. Call and reserve a seat
   C. Wait for the next event
   Ⓐ Ⓑ Ⓒ

Part 7 Case Study

18

Scenario: The coastal community of Oceanview is located on the shores of the Pacific Ocean. Oceanview is known for its laid-back, beachy vibe, and is a popular destination for tourists. Visitors can spend their days relaxing on the sandy beaches, surfing, or exploring the town's charming downtown area, filled with quaint boutiques and seafood restaurants.

Life in Oceanview is influenced by the unique challenges and opportunities of living near the ocean, such as severe weather events, and the need to adapt to rising sea levels. Oceanview has been experiencing more frequent and severe floods in recent years, and the residents are concerned about the impact on their homes and businesses. A group of residents has gathered to discuss the issue of rising sea levels and nuisance flooding and explore potential solutions.

A small group is talking about recent flooding. What problems are they having? What are some of their ideas?

Listen to their conversation and take notes in the space below.

A consultant has proposed these solutions to the people of Oceanview:

Solution 1

Elevating structures: One effective solution is to raise structures above the floodplain. One way is to elevate the foundations of buildings, another is to install flood vents to allow water to freely flow under the buildings.

Solution 2

Waterproofing buildings: A variety of techniques can be used to reduce the risk of damage to existing buildings. Some of these techniques are using different construction materials such as waterproof wallboards and flood-resistant windows, relocating electrical panels and HVAC systems, and removing downspouts.

Solution 3

Installing flood barriers: Another option is to install flood barriers, such as levees or sea walls, to protect against floodwaters. These barriers can be permanent or temporary, and can be used to protect individual buildings or entire communities.

Solution 4

Upgrading stormwater management systems: Improving the design and maintenance of stormwater management systems, such as catch basins and retention ponds, can help to reduce the likelihood and severity of nuisance flooding.

Solution 5

Building green infrastructure: Green infrastructure, such as green roofs, permeable pavement, and rain gardens, can help to reduce the impact of nuisance flooding by capturing and storing stormwater runoff. This can help to reduce the volume of water that flows into stormwater systems and ultimately leads to flooding.

Solution 6

Planning: Careful land use planning can also help to reduce the risk of nuisance flooding. For example, developing regulations that prohibit new development in flood-prone areas, or requiring that new developments include measures to manage stormwater runoff, can help to reduce the impact of flooding.

All of these solutions have advantages and disadvantages that need to be considered when choosing the best course of action for Oceanview. Choose ONE of the solutions and take notes.

With the members of your group, discuss each of the solutions using your notes. Together, choose ONE short-term solution and ONE long-term solution for Oceanview.

6 Zero Hunger

At the end of this unit, you will …

- ☐ understand how machine learning can be useful.
- ☐ understand why food waste is a difficult problem to solve.
- ☐ know how to avoid food waste.

Vocabulary Focus

A *Match the words (1-12) with the correct definitions (a-l). The first one has been done for you!*

1.	(g)	algorithm	7.	( )	landfill
2.	( )	assure	8.	( )	potential
3.	( )	complicate	9.	( )	prediction
4.	( )	consume	10.	( )	produce
5.	( )	groceries	11.	( )	promotion
6.	( )	inventory	12.	( )	scraps

a. a statement about what you think will happen
b. to make something more difficult to do or understand
c. the food that you buy in a supermarket
d. small pieces of food that are not eaten and thrown away
e. foods made by farms, especially fruits and vegetables
f. the goods a business has for sale
g. a set of rules that will help a computer answer a problem
h. a place where large amounts of garbage are buried
i. to eat or drink something
j. the ability to develop, achieve, or be successful
k. advertising to increase sales of a product or service
l. to make a promise or give confidence that something will happen

B *Complete the sentences with the words from MATCHING. You may need to change the word form.*

1. Every year, ______________ are made but many of them don't come true.
2. A lot of people like to buy their fresh ______________ from local farmers.
3. Sometimes overthinking ends up making problems more ______________.
4. The purpose of the law is to ______________ the safety of workers.
5. As better ______________ are developed, the process will be faster.

C *Write two original sentences using words from MATCHING to help you remember them. You may need to change the word form.*

1.
2.

Reading

19

Read this passage carefully and underline any unknown words.

Food Waste

In recent years, you may have heard the term "machine learning" and have wondered what it is exactly. Machine learning (ML) is a branch of *artificial intelligence which uses statistical methods and **algorithms** to learn from data in order to make **predictions** and decisions. Combined with the advances in computing technology, such as *quantum computers, ML will be able to complete tasks that are currently unimaginable.

Machine learning has a lot of **potential** to help with the growing problem of food waste. The United Nation reports that *931 million tons of food is thrown away each year with most of it ending up in **landfills**. The first level of food waste is at the retail level which is **grocery** stores and supermarkets. A large supermarket needs to have a large **inventory** of fresh **produce** such as fruits and vegetables to be competitive. Unfortunately, not everything is sold.

Imagine that you are in charge of the **produce** section in a supermarket. Ordering is a **complicated** process and you need to consider many things such as: how many are on the shelf, how quickly they sell, if demand will change because of upcoming promotions, and how reliable delivery will be. This process needs to be repeated for hundreds of different fruits and vegetables. The ordering process can be improved with the use of **inventory** software that has ML. Over time, the system learns and becomes better. It can help supermarkets optimize **inventory** levels by avoiding ordering too much which reduces wastage. Also, it can help keep customers happy by **assuring** that products are available when they are wanted and needed.

The second level of food waste is at the **consumer** level. As individuals, we can reduce food waste by taking simple steps. Perhaps an obvious step is to not buy unneeded foods. Before going to the supermarket, check your refrigerator to see what you actually have and what you need. Another step is to make your fresh **produce** last longer by setting the temperature of your refrigerator to around 5°C. Finally, if possible, *compost food **scraps** to use in the garden.

349 words: ____ minutes ____ seconds

Notes:

- artificial intelligence 人工知能
- quantum computer 量子コンピュータ
- 930 million tons – 843,681,808,200 kilograms
- compost コンポスト（生ごみかの堆肥化）

Understanding

A *Choose the best answer(s) to each question.*

1. Machine learning …
   a. can help you compost better.
   b. can make landfills more efficient.
   c. can solve complicated problems.
2. The first level of food waste …
   a. is the consumer one.
   b. is the manufacturing one.
   c. is the retail one.
3. Software can help stores …
   a. attract new customers.
   b. maintain ideal levels of goods.
   c. make produce last longer.

B *Answer the following questions. Use complete and grammatically correct sentences.*

1. What are some uses for machine learning?
2. Why is food waste a difficult problem for supermarkets to solve?
3. How can we reduce food waste in our homes?

C *The following statements have mistakes. Correct them.*

1. Machine learning can solve the problem of food waste entirely.
2. Supermarkets only waste food because they don't have enough inventory software with machine learning.
3. Setting the refrigerator to 0°C will make fresh produce last even longer.

D *These sentences were used in the READING. Circle the word that has a similar meaning.*

1. Machine learning is a **branch** of artificial intelligence which uses statistical methods and algorithms.
   a. field　　b. method　　c. system
2. Ordering is a complicated process and you need to **consider** many things.
   a. disregard　　b. keep in mind　　c. overlook
3. It can help supermarkets **optimize** inventory levels.
   a. diminish　　b. improve　　c. worsen
4. Perhaps an **obvious** step is to not buy unneeded foods.
   a. concealed　　b. questionable　　c. straightforward

Listening

A *Listen to each question and circle the letter of the best answer.* 20

1. What is the first level of food waste?
   a. households　　b. restaurants　　c. supermarkets
2. ______________________________?
   a. enormous　　b. modest　　c. wonderful
3. ______________________________?
   a. 2 degrees　　b. 5 degrees　　c. 8 degrees

B *Listen and write the missing words.* 21

1. My uncle works in the ________ section at the ________ supermarket.
2. If the inventory system is ________, it will be more ________.
3. They need to ________ that they sell ________ products at ________ prices.
4. Before you go ________________, you should ________________.
5. ______________________________.

Discussing

With a partner or in a small group, answer ONE of the following questions.

a. Where do you (or your family) usually buy your fruits and vegetables?
b. Would you consider composting your food scraps?
c. What can we do in our daily lives to reduce food waste?

Take your notes in the space below:

Sharing Information

Student A: Page 104
Student B: Page 116

Reviewing

Before you move on to the next unit, make sure you check all the boxes.

- ☐ I can explain why food waste is an important issue.
- ☐ I can list things that produce managers need to think about.
- ☐ I know at least one way to reduce food waste.

7 Sustainable Infrastructure

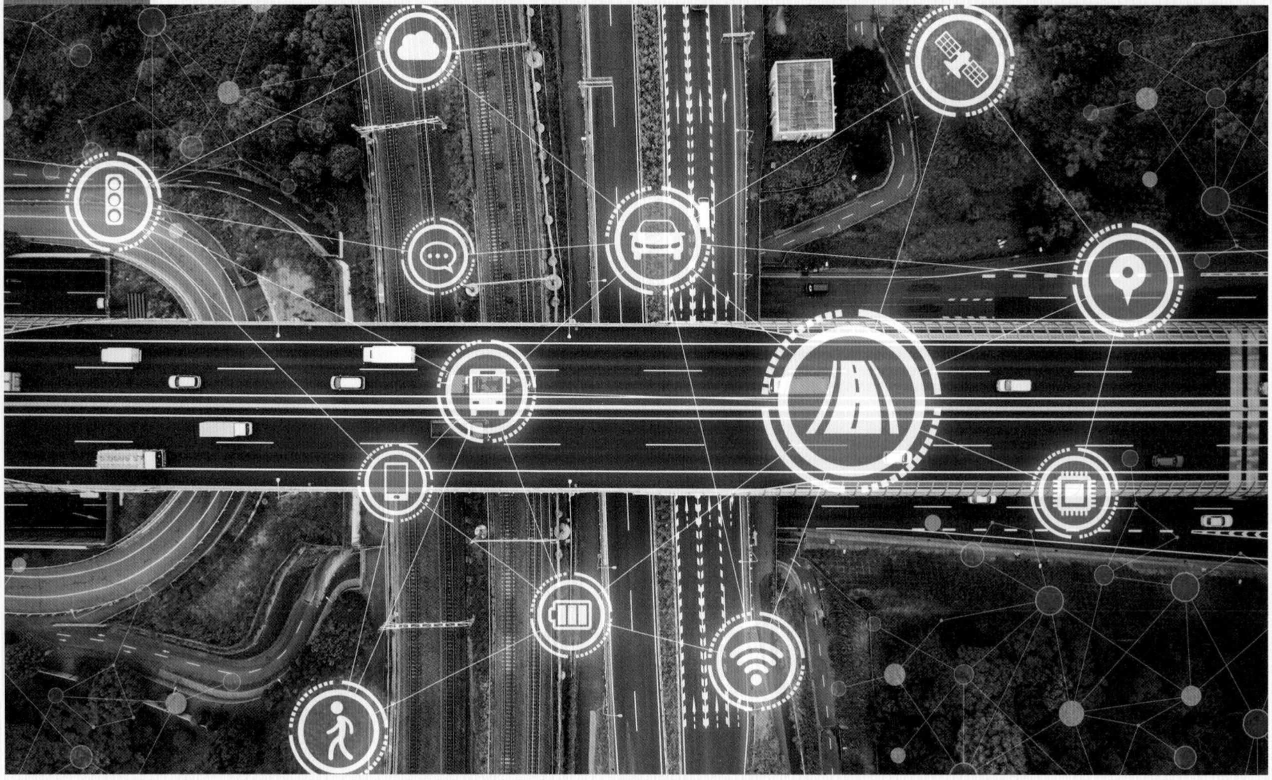

At the end of this unit, you will ...

- ☐ Understand the advantages and disadvantages of smart infrastructure.
- ☐ Be able to explain how smart infrastructure benefits the environment.
- ☐ Be able to explain how smart infrastructure improves the lives of citizens.

Vocabulary Focus

A *Match the words (1-12) with the correct definitions (a-l). The first one has been done for you!*

1.	(h)	absorb	7.	( )	hybrid
2.	( )	acquisition	8.	( )	optimize
3.	( )	analytics	9.	( )	relocation
4.	( )	controversial	10.	( )	sensors
5.	( )	disrupt	11.	( )	specialize
6.	( )	efficiency	12.	( )	urbanization

a. something that combines two or more different things or has characteristics of two different things
b. to make something as effective or efficient as possible
c. something that people strongly disagree about or have different opinions on
d. to interrupt or change the normal course of something
e. the act of getting something or gaining ownership of something
f. the process of more and more people living in cities and urban areas
g. being able to do something in a way that saves time, money, or resources
h. to take in or soak up something
i. using data or information to better understand something or make decisions
j. devices that can detect or measure physical properties such as temperature, light, sound, or movement
k. moving to a new place or moving something to a new location
l. to focus on one particular area or subject and become an expert in it

B *Complete the sentences with the words from MATCHING. You may need to change the word form.*

1. My new car is a(n) ________________, which means it uses both gasoline and electricity to run.
2. To ________________ my morning routine, I set my alarm clock earlier so I have more time to get ready.
3. The ________________ in my smartwatch track my steps, heart rate, and sleep patterns.
4. She decided to ________________ in dentistry, so she went to dental school to become a dentist.
5. ________________ is the process of people moving from rural areas to cities, resulting in the growth of urban areas.

C *Write two original sentences using words from MATCHING to help you remember them.*

1.
2.

Reading

22

Read this passage carefully and underline any unknown words.

Cities of the Future

Sustainable infrastructure refers to the design and construction of buildings, transportation systems, and other structures in a way that is environmentally friendly and resource-**efficient**. In cities of the future, sustainable infrastructure will include a variety of features and technologies to reduce the environmental impact of **urbanization** while improving the quality of life for residents.

One key aspect of sustainable infrastructure is the use of renewable energy sources to power buildings and transportation systems. These sources could be solar panels, wind turbines, or other clean energy technologies. In addition, sustainable infrastructure may include the use of green roofs, which are roofs that are covered with vegetation and help to **absorb** rainwater, reduce *heat island effect, and improve air quality.

Another important aspect is the use of **efficient** and sustainable transportation systems, such as electric or **hybrid** vehicles, bike-sharing programs, and public transportation systems that use clean energy sources. These systems can help to reduce air pollution and greenhouse gas emissions, while also providing convenient and cost-effective transportation options for the people.

Sustainable infrastructure may also include the use of smart technologies, such as sensors and data **analytics**, to monitor and **optimize** the performance of buildings and transportation systems. This can help to improve energy **efficiency** and reduce resource consumption, while also providing valuable data that can be used to inform decision-making and planning.

One potential downside of sustainable infrastructure is that it is often more expensive to build and maintain than traditional infrastructure. This can be a barrier for governments and organizations that may not have the necessary financial resources. Additionally, the construction of sustainable infrastructure projects may also take longer to complete due to the need for **specialized** materials and technologies, which can cause delays and **disrupt** regular activities in the area where the infrastructure is being built. Finally, sustainable infrastructure may require the acquisition of land or the relocation of existing communities, which can be **controversial** and emotional.

Sustainable infrastructure is an important part of creating livable, healthy, and environmentally friendly cities of the future. By designing and building cities with a focus on sustainability, we can help to reduce our impact on the environment and create a more sustainable future for all.

364 words: ____ minutes ____ seconds

Notes:

- **heat island effect** ヒートアイランド現象

Understanding

A *Choose the best answer(s) to each question.*

1. What is sustainable infrastructure?
   a. The design and construction of buildings, transportation systems, and other structures in a way that is environmentally friendly and resource-efficient.
   b. The design and construction of buildings, transportation systems, and other structures in a way that is expensive and time-consuming.
   c. The design and construction of buildings, transportation systems, and other structures in a way that is not environmentally friendly.

2. What is an example of a sustainable transportation system?
   a. diesel vehicles b. gasoline vehicles c. hybrid vehicles

3. What is a potential downside of sustainable infrastructure?
   a. It is faster and easier to build than traditional infrastructure.
   b. It is not cost-effective.
   c. It requires the use of non-renewable energy sources.

B *Answer the following questions. Use complete and grammatically correct sentences.*

1. What are some examples of smart technologies?

2. What are some potential benefits of using smart technologies in sustainable infrastructure?

3. What are some potential challenges associated with building sustainable infrastructure?

C *The following statements have mistakes. Correct them.*

1. Sustainable infrastructure only involves the use of renewable energy sources.

2. Sustainable infrastructure is always cheaper and quicker to build than traditional infrastructure.

3. Relocating existing communities is always necessary for sustainable infrastructure projects.

D *These sentences were used in the READING. Circle the word that has a similar meaning.*

1. Sustainable infrastructure refers to the **design** and construction of buildings.
   a. designate b. destroy c. plan
2. One **key** aspect of sustainable infrastructure is the use of renewable energy sources.
   a. crucial b. normal c. trivial
3. These systems can also **provide** convenient and cost-effective transportation options for residents.
   a. deprive b. offer c. provoke
4. Sustainable infrastructure may require the **acquisition** of land or the relocation of existing communities.
   c. accusation b. acquaintance c. purchase

Listening

A *Listen to each question and circle the letter of the best answer.* 23

1. How do smart infrastructure projects optimize energy usage?
   a. offering cost-effective transportation
   b. reducing the environmental impact
   c. using sensors to monitor and optimize it
2. ____?
   a. bike-sharing b. green roofs c. sensors
3. ____?
   a. it is cheaper b. it is more expensive c. it takes longer to build

B *Listen and write the missing words.* 24

1. Plants ____________ and convert it into energy through photosynthesis.
2. The __________ new policy sparked heated __________ among politicians.
3. __________ is considering ____________________ in order to expand its market reach.
4. ____________ of the new highway will ______________________ and wildlife __________.
5. ____
   ________________________.

Discussing

With a partner or in a small group, answer ONE of the following questions.

a. What is smart infrastructure?
b. What are some examples of smart infrastructure in your city?
c. How can smart infrastructure help make our cities more sustainable and livable?

Take your notes in the space below:

Sharing Information

Student A: Page 105
Student B: Page 117

Reviewing

Before you move on to the next unit, make sure you check all the boxes.

- ☐ I understand the advantages and disadvantages of smart infrastructure.
- ☐ I can explain how smart infrastructure benefits the environment.
- ☐ I can explain how smart infrastructure improves the lives of citizens.

8 Clean Energy

At the end of this unit, you will …

- ☐ understand limitations on renewable energy sources.
- ☐ understand why more efficient batteries are necessary.
- ☐ understand some ways to reduce energy consumption.

Vocabulary Focus

A *Match the words (1-12) with the correct definitions (a-l). The first one has been done for you!*

1.	(c)	aid	7.	( )	peak
2.	( )	backup	8.	( )	plenty
3.	( )	efficiently	9.	( )	primary
4.	( )	grid	10.	( )	regularly
5.	( )	independence	11.	( )	reliance
6.	( )	outlet	12.	( )	scientist

a. The highest point or value of something
b. A person who has expert knowledge in one of the sciences
c. To provide help or support to someone or something
d. A large amount of something
e. The main or most used thing among others
f. Something done many times with the same time interval
g. Do not depend on someone or something
h. Something that can be used if necessary
i. To avoid waste
j. A network that delivers electricity to consumers in a large area
k. A place on a wall where you can connect electrical things to power
l. To need or depend on something or someone

B *Complete the sentences with the words from MATCHING. You may need to change the word form.*

1. In the case of an emergency, we may need ________________ from strangers.
2. The ________________ cause of the accident was carelessness.
3. After training seriously for over a year, the athlete was in ________________ condition.
4. Many young people want to be ________________ and make their own decisions.
5. To ensure that your car is safe and reliable, you should have it maintained ________________.

C *Write two original sentences using words from MATCHING to help you remember them. You may need to change the word form.*

1.
2.

Reading

25

Read this passage carefully and underline any unknown words.

A Bright Future for Energy

As technology advances, more energy is necessary to keep our *gadgets working. Humanity is looking for cleaner ways to generate electricity and more **efficient** ways to store it. Renewable energy sources such as solar, wind, and hydroelectricity are getting cheaper and more **efficient**, but they do not produce enough power at **peak** times of the day or at night when everyone needs their lights on. This is the reason why renewables need a **backup**. There are several technologies that can serve as a **backup** source of energy when using renewable energy and the most promising one is batteries.

Batteries have been around for a long time now, but they are still not quite as **efficient** as they could be. In order to improve them, scientists are looking into newer materials that can store larger amounts of electricity while also being less expensive to produce. Storing energy in batteries can help us use renewable energy sources more **efficiently**. For example, on cloudy days when solar panels are not producing much energy, batteries can provide the required electricity to run the machines that make our lives easier.

New types of batteries also make life easier for people who live in rural areas where there is no access to a power **grid**. Those who live far from urban areas may have trouble charging their phones or other devices **regularly** if they do not have an **outlet** nearby or a power **backup** system in case something happens. Another big advantage of batteries is that they can be used by households and **aid** communities hit by natural disasters.

There are **plenty** of options for generating power from renewable sources and many countries are investing heavily because it provides them with a lot of benefits: lower costs for consumers and businesses; job creation; reduced **reliance** on foreign oil imports; carbon emissions cuts; and greater energy **independence**. The use of *fossil fuels for generating power is slowly decreasing and as advances in technology make batteries even lighter and more **efficient**, renewable sources might soon be used as a **primary** source for us all.

346 words: ____ minutes ____ seconds

Notes:
- gadget 電子機器
- fossil fuels 化石燃料

Understanding

A *Choose the best answer(s) to each question.*

1. Renewable energy …
   a. can supply all the electricity we need.
   b. is something scientists have been researching.
   c. is the primary source in most places of the world.
2. People in urban areas …
   a. do not have much trouble charging their phones.
   b. have better efficiency.
   c. have trouble charging their phones.
3. Many countries are investing in renewable energy …
   a. because batteries have been around for a long time.
   b. because humanity needs it.
   c. because it allows them to be more independent.

B *Answer the following questions. Use complete and grammatically correct sentences.*

1. Why do we need more energy?

2. What is a problem with renewable energy sources?

3. How can we improve the efficiency of batteries?

C *The following statements have mistakes. Correct them.*

1. Renewable energy sources are producing enough power at peak times.

2. Some countries are afraid of renewables because there are just a few options.

3. It looks like renewable energy will be used only in our homes in the future.

D *These sentences were used in the READING. Circle the word that has a similar meaning.*

1. Humanity is looking for cleaner ways to **generate** electricity.
   a. create   b. find   c. improve
2. They don't produce enough power at **peak** times.
   a. look quickly   b. most necessary   c. mountain top
3. Those who live far from **urban** areas may have trouble charging their phones.
   a. crowded   b. important   c. near the sea
4. It **reduces** reliance on foreign oil imports.
   a. compliments   b. diminishes   c. enhances

Listening

A *Listen to each question and circle the letter of the best answer.* 26

1. New types of batteries can help people living in which areas?
   a. at the beach
   b. in the city
   c. in the countryside
2. ____?
   a. a backup system
   b. for disaster aid and relief
   c. to connect to the grid
3. ____?
   a. because energy from fossil fuels is decreasing
   b. because it costs less
   c. because they need to import less oil

B *Listen and write the missing words.* 27

1. Before we can switch to ______________________, a lot of research must be done.
2. Being in direct __________ makes a solar panel more efficient.
3. As the price of electricity __________, many people ______________ buying battery __________.
4. Nowadays, companies selling ______________________________.
5. ____.

Discussing

With a partner or in a small group, answer ONE of the following questions.

a. How much electricity does your household consume?
b. Do you have anything in your home that runs 24 hours a day?
c. Without electricity at night, how would your daily life change?

Take your notes in the space below:

Sharing Information

Student A: Page 106
Student B: Page 118

Reviewing

Before you move on to the next unit, make sure you check all the boxes.

☐ I can explain why backup systems are necessary.
☐ I understand the limitations of renewable energy production.
☐ I know at least one way to reduce my energy consumption.

9 Remote Work

At the end of this unit, you will ...

- ☐ understand why remote work is possible.
- ☐ understand the advantages and disadvantages of remote work.
- ☐ understand how remote work changed the way people work.

Vocabulary Focus

A *Match the words (1-12) with the correct definitions (a-l). The first one has been done for you!*

1.	(e)	advancements	7.	( )	physically
2.	( )	anticipate	8.	( )	plentiful
3.	( )	collaborate	9.	( )	predictable
4.	( )	commute	10.	( )	regardless
5.	( )	decline	11.	( )	smoothly
6.	( )	flexibility	12.	( )	telework

a. to think about something that might happen in the future
b. working from home instead of going to an office or a workplace
c. when a number or need for something goes down
d. doing something or not doing something, without being affected by other things
e. improvements or progress in something
f. traveling to and from work or school every day
g. when something happens the way you expect it to
h. being able to change your plans or schedule if needed
i. working together with other people to get something done
j. something that relates to your body and movement
k. something happens easily and without any problems
l. there is a lot of something

B *Complete the sentences with the words from MATCHING. You may need to change the word form.*

1. I always try to ________________ what my little sister will need before she asks for it.
2. Since the pandemic started, many people have started doing ________________ from home instead of going to the office.
3. The number of bees has been in ________________ in recent years, which is causing concern for the health of our environment.
4. ________________ of the weather, I always try to get outside and play soccer with my friends.
5. The ________________ in medicine in the last few decades have made it possible to cure many illnesses that were once deadly.

C *Write two original sentences using words from MATCHING to help you remember them.*

1.
2.

Reading

28

Read this passage carefully and underline any unknown words.

Telework

These days, more companies are allowing and even encouraging employees to work remotely (**telework**) as it becomes easier and more affordable due to technological **advancements**. In fact, more than half of American companies regularly allow some amount of telework.

There are numerous benefits of **teleworking** for employees. For example, they can work from home or even while on vacation and still meet their work responsibilities. Also, they can spend more time at home because there is no need to **commute** to their workplaces. This additional time that is saved can be used for other activities. Some people prefer working a set number of hours each week and want a **predictable** schedule so they can plan their lives around it. Others enjoy the **flexibility** that **teleworking** provides and would rather work when they want and as long as they want, **regardless** of the time of day or day of the week.

There are also advantages for companies. They can have employees located anywhere in the country or even overseas without having to worry about additional costs. Instead of paying for transportation and accommodation for employees to attend business meetings, they can be held online. Companies can also have teams of employees who live in different parts of the world **collaborate** on projects through video calls or chat instead of having face-to-face meetings.

One thing that is unclear about this trend is whether it will result in higher wages for workers with specialized skills or a **decline** for those who lack them. Also, many companies have been looking for ways to keep their employees busy while they are away from their desks. This is because some companies have realized that there is a need for workers to be **physically** present in the office in order for things to run **smoothly**. As a result, many jobs that were once considered as "on-call" or "remote" are now considered essential full-time positions with benefits and paid holidays.

The benefits of **telework** are **plentiful** to both companies and their employees. The trend of working from home has become popular and will continue to be attractive to many people. In the future, we **anticipate** that even more people will want to work for companies that allow employees to work from home.

374 words: ____ minutes ____ seconds

Understanding

A *Choose the best answer(s) to each question.*

1. What are some advantages of teleworking for employees?
   a. They can save time on commuting.
   b. They can work more hours than in the office.
   c. They have to work on weekends.

2. Why do companies prefer online business meetings?
   a. To avoid talking to their employees
   b. To ensure employees are physically present in the office
   c. To save money on transportation and accommodation

3. What is one thing that is unclear about the trend of teleworking?
   a. Whether it will lead to higher wages for workers with specialized skills.
   b. Whether it will make employees work more hours.
   c. Whether it will only benefit companies and not their employees.

B *Answer the following questions. Use complete and grammatically correct sentences.*

1. What are some of the benefits for employees who work from home?

2. How do online business meetings benefit companies?

3. What are some of the potential drawbacks of teleworking?

C *The following statements have mistakes. Correct them.*

1. Teleworking is bad for employees because they have to work longer hours.

2. Companies don't need face-to-face meetings anymore because they can save money with online meetings.

3. In the future everyone will be teleworking.

D *These sentences were used in the READING. Circle the word that has a similar meaning.*

1. There are **numerous** benefits of teleworking for employees.
   a. abundant　　b. numerator　　c. scarce
2. Some people want a **predictable** schedule.
   a. expected　　b. preoccupation　　c. surprising
3. Some companies have **realized** that there is a need for workers to be physically present.
   a. neglected　　b. promised　　c. recognized
4. We **anticipate** that even more people will want to work for companies that allow employees to work from home.
   a. disregard　　b. foresee　　c. overlook

Listening

A *Listen to each question and circle the letter of the best answer.* 29

1. According to the text, why are more companies allowing telework?
   a. Because technological advancements have made teleworking easier and more affordable
   b. Because they want to decrease employee productivity
   c. Because they want to save money on employee salaries
2. ______________________________?
   a. They can work from home or while on vacation
   b. They can work only during set hours each week
   c. They have to commute to work, which can be time-consuming
3. ______________________________?
   a. They can have employees located anywhere without additional costs
   b. They can have fewer employees
   c. They can save money on employee salaries

B *Listen and write the missing words.* 30

1. The harvest was __________ this year, and we had enough to feed the entire village.
2. Her __________ behavior made it easy for others to know how she __________.
3. He was ______________ to run a marathon due to ______________.
4. The __________ was able to ____________________ on the project using ______________ tools.
5. ____.

Discussing

With a partner or in a small group, answer ONE of the following questions.

a. What jobs are best suited for telework?
b. Do you think working from home would be fun? Why or why not?
c. What are some advantages of working from home? What are some disadvantages?

Take your notes in the space below:

Sharing Information

Student A: Page 107
Student B: Page 119

Reviewing

Before you move on to the next unit, make sure you check all the boxes.

- ☐ I understand why remote work is possible.
- ☐ I understand the advantages and disadvantages of remote work.
- ☐ I understand how remote work changed the way people work.

10 Review: Units 6-9

Part 1 Photographs

31

You will hear three short statements. Look at the picture and choose the statement that best describes what you see in the picture.

1.

Ⓐ Ⓑ Ⓒ

2.

Ⓐ Ⓑ Ⓒ

3.

Ⓐ Ⓑ Ⓒ

4.

Ⓐ Ⓑ Ⓒ

Part 2 Question-Response

32

You will hear a question or statement followed by three responses. Choose the best response.

1. Mark your answer. Ⓐ Ⓑ Ⓒ
2. Mark your answer. Ⓐ Ⓑ Ⓒ
3. Mark your answer. Ⓐ Ⓑ Ⓒ
4. Mark your answer. Ⓐ Ⓑ Ⓒ
5. Mark your answer. Ⓐ Ⓑ Ⓒ
6. Mark your answer. Ⓐ Ⓑ Ⓒ

Part 3 Short Conversations

33

You will hear short conversations between two people. Choose the best answer to each of the three questions.

Dialogue 1

1. Who most likely are the speakers?
   A. A couple B. Colleagues C. Friends Ⓐ Ⓑ Ⓒ
2. How does the woman feel about teleworking?
   A. She doesn't like it. B. She enjoys it.
   C. She finds it challenging. Ⓐ Ⓑ Ⓒ
3. What is the main challenge of teleworking according to the woman?
   A. Having less flexibility in her schedule B. Having to commute more
   C. Staying motivated Ⓐ Ⓑ Ⓒ

Dialogue 2

1. Who most likely are the speakers?
   A. A couple B. Colleagues C. Friends Ⓐ Ⓑ Ⓒ
2. What are they talking about?
   A. Apps B. Groceries C. Refrigerators Ⓐ Ⓑ Ⓒ
3. What are they likely to do next?
   A. Check their budget B. Do some research C. Order groceries Ⓐ Ⓑ Ⓒ

Part 4 Short Talk

34

You will hear a short talk. Choose the best answer to each of the three questions.

1. What was the initial goal of the 100-Mile Diet?
   A. To encourage people to eat more exotic foods
   B. To increase the amount of processed foods in people's diets
   C. To promote a vegetarian lifestyle
   D. To reduce the carbon footprint of meals Ⓐ Ⓑ Ⓒ Ⓓ
2. What is the benefit of eating seasonally?
   A. It provides access to fresher and more nutritious foods.
   B. It supports local farmers
   C. It's cheaper than eating out
   D. It's easier to find food in the grocery store Ⓐ Ⓑ Ⓒ Ⓓ
3. Which of the following is NOT an example of a locally sourced food?
   A. A loaf of bread made from locally grown wheat
   B. A steak from a nearby farm
   C. A tomato grown in your backyard
   D. An avocado imported from Mexico Ⓐ Ⓑ Ⓒ Ⓓ

Part 5 Text Completion

Four words or phrases are missing in the text. Choose the best answers to complete the text.

Are you tired of being (1) from the world when you are on a camping trip? Need backup power for your home or office in case of emergencies? Introducing the perfect companion for all of your outdoor adventures - the Wanderer Power Station.

- The Wanderer is a (2) portable battery with a user-friendly design that is easy to carry.
- Eco-friendly and quiet, the Wanderer can safely provide power anywhere, the power you need, unlike gas generators.

The Wanderer is specially designed for outdoor use, with a durable and rugged construction that can (3) the toughest weather conditions. It has a robust 290Wh (20.3Ah) lithium battery which means you can power all your appliances and electronic devices. For example, the Wanderer can charge your smartphone (29 times), drone (6 times), laptop (4 times) or run appliances like a mini refrigerator (19 hours), television (4 hours) and a desk lamp (23 hours).

With its long battery life, you won't have to worry about running out of power during your trip. And when you do need to recharge, the Wanderer can be easily charged in one of three ways: solar (5 hours - requires an (4) Helios Saga 100 sold separately), AC outlet (6 hours) and car charging (6.5 hours). This means you can charge it up in any way that's convenient for you, even when you're on the go.

Are you interested in learning more about the Wanderer Power Station? Call our award-winning customer service at 1-800-BAT-TERY (1-800-228-8379) to learn more.

1. A. disconnected B. joined
   C. linked D. united (A) (B) (C) (D)

2. A. delicate B. durable
   C. flimsy D. vulnerable (A) (B) (C) (D)

3. A. collapse B. endure
   C. surrender D. yield (A) (B) (C) (D)

4. A. indispensable B. mandatory
   C. obligatory D. optional (A) (B) (C) (D)

Part 6 Reading Comprehension

Read the following text. Choose the best answer to each question.

Masdar City, a modern and futuristic urban development project that covers an area of six square kilometers, is located in Abu Dhabi, the capital city of the United Arab Emirates. It was designed to be a sustainable and eco-friendly city, with the goal of achieving zero carbon emissions and zero waste.

The city was announced in 2006 and construction is expected to be completed by 2030. Once completed, it will be home to between 40,000 and 50,000 residents. It is expected that 1,500 companies will locate there and provide over 60,000 jobs.

An important aspect of this project is the use of sustainable construction. The buildings are constructed with eco-friendly materials such as low-carbon cement and 90% recycled aluminum. The buildings have been designed to maximize natural light and ventilation, while minimizing energy consumption. The eco-villas for the residents have been designed to produce more energy than they consume by using high-performance solar photovoltaic (PV) panels. A rainwater collection system, along with low-demand water fittings help reduce water use by 35%.

Masdar City is a pedestrian-friendly city that encourages walking and avoids the use of cars. It has narrow streets that run in directions that take advantage of air currents which reduce heat and promote walking and cycling. It also has unique clean technology transportation systems, such as automated electric cars that run on magnetic tracks called Personal Rapid Transit, and autonomous e-buses which reduce carbon emissions and traffic congestion.

1. Where is this text likely to be found?
   A. A flyer
   B. A magazine
   C. An encyclopedia
   Ⓐ Ⓑ Ⓒ
2. What is Masdar City?
   A. A city built in Dubai with modern and futuristic features
   B. A city that produces a lot of waste and carbon emissions
   C. A city with buildings made of eco-friendly materials
   Ⓐ Ⓑ Ⓒ
3. What is the main objective of Masdar City?
   A. To achieve zero carbon emissions and zero waste
   B. To encourage more people to walk
   C. To maximize the use of public transportation
   Ⓐ Ⓑ Ⓒ
4. What transportation methods are available?
   A. Autonomous e-buses
   B. Automated electric cars
   C. Diesel-powered buses
   Ⓐ Ⓑ Ⓒ

Part 7 Case Study

35

Scenario: The city of Oakwood is a medium-sized city of approximately 200,000 people. For decades, Oakwood was a thriving center of manufacturing and agriculture, with factories producing everything from farm equipment to car parts and fertile farmland surrounding the town.

In recent years, however, many of the factories and farms in Oakwood have closed down, leaving the community struggling to make ends meet. The town council recognizes that something needs to be done to revitalize the area, and they believe that creating an ecodistrict is the key.

A small group of residents is talking with a consultant about the possibility of an ecodistrict. What are their concerns? What is the reaction of the residents?

Listen to their conversation and take notes in the space below.

The consultant has proposed several initiatives to be implemented over the next 5-10 years.

Proposed Initiatives

Initiative 1

Retrofitting factories and farms: Factories will require that they implement noise-reducing measures, such as installing sound barriers and lowering machinery noise. Farmers will be encouraged to adopt sustainable agriculture practices. This initiative will include providing education and training to farmers and offering financial incentives for those who participate. Assuming there are around 20 factories and farms in Oakwood that require retrofitting, the total cost could range from $8 million to $10 million.

Initiative 2

Financing: This initiative will include offering low-interest loans and grants to homeowners who wish to make energy-efficient improvements such as installing insulation or upgrading to energy-efficient appliances. The estimated cost of this initiative is $10 million.

Initiative 3

Implementing green roofs on all buildings: The cost of installing green roofs varies based on the size and design of the roof. However, a rough estimate of implementing green roofs on all buildings in Oakwood could range from $5 million to $8 million.

Initiative 4

Upgrading the transportation system: Upgrading the transportation system would involve replacing the existing vehicles with electric ones, building charging stations, and improving public transport. The cost for each electric bus can range from $800,000 to $1.5 million. Assuming the cost of building charging stations would be around $100,000 per station, and the cost of upgrading public transport would be around $2 million, the total cost for upgrading the transportation system in Oakwood could be around $94 million.

Initiative 5

Establishing community gardens and green spaces: The average cost of developing a community garden is around $2,500-$3,500 per 100 square meters. Assuming the total area for community gardens and green spaces would be around 50 acres (200,000 square meters), the cost of establishing these spaces in Oakwood could range from $10 million to $15 million.

All of these initiatives have advantages and disadvantages that need to be considered. Choose ONE of the initiatives and take notes.

With the members of your group, discuss each of the initiatives using your notes. Together, choose TWO initiatives for Oakwood.

11 Quality Education for All

At the end of this unit, you will ...

- ☐ understand the importance of education for the economy.
- ☐ understand methods to provide education to remote areas.
- ☐ understand how education is changing.

Vocabulary Focus

A *Match the words (1-12) with the correct definitions (a-l). The first one has been done for you!*

1.	(j)	approximately	7.	( )	literally
2.	( )	consist	8.	( )	mandatory
3.	( )	delivery	9.	( )	priority
4.	( )	entrepreneur	10.	( )	robust
5.	( )	ingenious	11.	( )	shelter
6.	( )	landmark	12.	( )	subsidy

a. something that is more important than other things
b. a place to live and stay
c. something you can see from a distance that helps you know your location
d. to emphasize that something is really true
e. strong and healthy
f. the process of sending something from one place to another
g. to be made up from things listed
h. money paid by the government to reduce costs so prices are lower
i. a person with a lot of clever, original ideas
j. close in number or amount but not exact
k. a person who makes money by starting businesses
l. required by law

B *Complete the sentences with the words from MATCHING. You may need to change the word form.*

1. ______________ 8,000 fans waited in the airport for their favorite band to arrive.
2. The energetic and ______________ boy spent his summer vacation playing outdoors.
3. The ______________ inventor is always coming up with new ideas and gadgets.
4. Because of the generous ______________, we decided to buy solar panels for the house.
5. Excellent customer service is a ______________ at the popular family restaurant.

C *Write two original sentences using words from MATCHING to help you remember them. You may need to change the word form.*

1.
2.

Reading

36

Read this passage carefully and underline any unknown words.

Quality Education for All

In many *industrialized countries, education is **mandatory** and is free or heavily **subsidized**. Why is such a **priority** placed on education? A country needs a well-educated workforce in order to have a **robust** economy. For individuals, education opens many doors such as better paying jobs. It has been reported that each year of education adds **approximately** 9% to the hourly wage earned. A stable job allows a person to meet their basic needs such as food, **shelter**, and clothing. Of course, having a higher income allows people to buy things they want to make their lives more comfortable and enjoyable. Unfortunately, many low and middle income countries have high levels of "Learning Poverty" which is the number of 10-year-old children who cannot read a simple story.

Technology can provide many tools to deal with this problem. A distributed learning system uses multiple modes of **delivery** to provide education. For students with access to reliable Internet, many modes are possible. However, in poor and remote areas, different solutions are required. Although not modern technologies, radio and television are being used to reach children who are unable to attend school. In Africa, one **ingenious entrepreneur** has developed a creative solution. It is a low-cost system that **consists** of a microcomputer, *router, and a power supply with a solar panel. These systems are **literally** being installed in large trees and **landmarks** so they have been called "Trees of Knowledge." Because many people in remote African villages have limited Internet access, this system was designed to work with any wifi-enabled device. Each of these systems is filled with free educational materials such as video lectures and learning materials. The systems can also provide health information and life-skills guides.

In addition to providing education to larger numbers of people, technology is actually changing how education is delivered. In the past, the main form of instruction was in traditional classrooms. Naturally, students needed to physically attend the classes. However, distributed learning provides students with alternatives. Students can attend classes remotely with the use of videoconferencing software. Also, courses can be designed so that students can study whenever they want, not just when the class is held. Even more interesting is that you can find online courses on almost any subject that you can imagine!

378 words: ____ minutes ____ seconds

Notes:

- industrialized country 先進国
- router ルーター

Understanding

A *Choose the best answer(s) to each question.*

1. What does "Learning Poverty" measure?
   a. How many children are unable to read.
   b. How many children cannot go to school.
   c. How many children go to bad schools.

2. What is the main feature of distributed learning?
   a. It uses only the Internet.
   b. It uses several delivery modes.
   c. It uses the latest forms of technology.

3. Which older technologies are used in remote areas?
   a. fax machines
   b. radio
   c. television

B *Answer the following questions. Use complete and grammatically correct sentences.*

1. Why is education a priority in many countries?

2. What are some of the benefits of education?

3. What is a "Tree of Knowledge"?

C *The following statements have mistakes. Correct them.*

1. In poor and remote areas, the same solutions can be used.

2. Each year of education adds exactly 9% to the annual salary earned.

3. Someday students will be able to attend classes remotely with videoconferencing.

D *These sentences were used in the READING. Circle the word that has a similar meaning.*

1. Education opens many **doors** such as better paying jobs.
   a. careers　　b. possibilities　　c. windows
2. Technology can provide many **tools** to deal with this problem
   a. computers　　b. data　　c. options
3. For students with access to **reliable** Internet, many modes are possible
   a. expensive　　b. resonant　　c. trustworthy
4. Students can study **whenever** they want
   a. anyhow　　b. anytime　　c. anywhere

Listening

A *Listen to each question and circle the letter of the best answer.* 37

1. What age of children's reading ability is measured by "Learning Poverty"?
   a. 7　　b. 10　　c. 12
2. ______________________________?
   a. clothing　　b. entertainment　　c. housing
3. ______________________________?
   a. obstacles　　b. options　　c. problems

B *Listen and write the missing words.* 38

1. Since I upgraded my Internet service, I __________ remote classes.
2. Not all television programs are ______________, some are educational.
3. We can learn __________ from free ______________ on the Internet.
4. I __________ how to use ____________ and spreadsheets __________.
5. ______________________________________.

Discussing

With a partner or in a small group, answer ONE of the following questions.

a. What is a skill that you taught yourself? How did you do it?
b. If you could learn anything, what would it be?
c. Which do you prefer, learning alone or with others?

Take your notes in the space below:

Sharing Information

Student A: Page 108
Student B: Page 120

Reviewing

Before you move on to the next unit, make sure you check all the boxes.

☐ I can explain how education improves the lives of people.
☐ I can describe some initiatives to provide education in rural areas.
☐ I can list some ways that education is changing.

12 Reducing Inequalities

At the end of this unit, you will ...

- ☐ understand some of the impacts of income equality.
- ☐ understand the importance of digital identities.
- ☐ be able to explain how digital IDs can be used.

Vocabulary Focus

A *Match the words (1-12) with the correct definitions (a-l). The first one has been done for you!*

1.	(i)	address	7.	( )	inequality
2.	( )	contribute	8.	( )	integrate
3.	( )	distribute	9.	( )	key
4.	( )	extreme	10.	( )	migrate
5.	( )	feasible	11.	( )	transfer
6.	( )	identity	12.	( )	verify

a. an unfair difference between groups of people
b. to share something with a number of people
c. to be one of the causes of something
d. to move from one place to live or work in another
e. serious or severe
f. to check that something is correct
g. to combine two or more things
h. the most important thing that allows you to do something
i. taking action to make things better
j. possible or likely to be done
k. who someone is
l. to send something from one place to another

B *Complete the sentences with the words from MATCHING. You may need to change the word form.*

1. Because of changes in the economy, the workers ________ to a larger city.
2. Did you remember to ________ the contents before you signed the document?
3. The famous actress said that the ________ to her success was dedication.
4. Before the end of the day, I need to ________ money to pay the bill.
5. The lack of a detailed plan ________ to the failure of the project.

C *Write two original sentences using words from MATCHING to help you remember them. You may need to change the word form.*

1.
2.

Reading

39

Read this passage carefully and underline any unknown words.

Digital Identities

Our world is filled with many **inequalities** with income **inequalities** being one of the biggest. Income **inequality** occurs when the income within a population, such as a community or country, is unevenly **distributed**. It has been reported that the top 10% have 75% of the world's wealth but the bottom 50% have only 2%. The impact of this can be felt on a daily basis as people compare themselves to others and society. Technology can help address some of the factors that **contribute** to income **inequality**.

Location has an influence on income. For people who live in rural or remote areas, there are limited opportunities for work. Also, the wages tend to be lower than those in urban areas. For these reasons, many young people **migrate** to cities for work opportunities. However, advances in Internet technology, such as *video conferencing and *cloud services, have made it possible for people to work from anywhere with reliable Internet access. This provides access to better paying jobs for those who are unable to move.

For people living in **extreme** poverty, remote work is not **feasible**. However, technology can also improve their lives. In many low- and middle-income countries, the governments are providing their citizens with digital **identities** which allow them to access government and private services. The e-ID Card, used in Nigeria, is a good example of how useful and life changing digital **identities** can be. This smart card has a *silicon ***integrated** circuit (IC) chip which securely stores a variety of information about the cardholder. As the name of the card suggests, it holds **key** information such as name, address, identification number, and fingerprints. Because the information contained by the card has been **verified**, the user can do useful things such as opening a bank account. Another benefit of the e-iD Card is that it can be used for **transferring** money and making payments for goods and services. It also has a digital signature which can be used for contracts, applications, and documents. Finally, the card can be used like an international passport. In the future, the card will be even more useful when it can be used for health insurance, public transportation, and voting.

Although quite different, remote work and digital **identities** have a lot of potential to **address** the issues that are created by income **inequality**.

387 words: ____ minutes ____ seconds

Notes:
- video conferencing ビデオ会議
- cloud services クラウドサービス
- silicon シリコン
- integrated circuit chip 集積回路（IC）チップ

Understanding

A *Choose the best answer(s) to each question.*

1. Why do many young people move to cities?
   a. to find better jobs
   b. to have Internet access
   c. to make more money

2. What is remote work?
   a. using cloud services to work from anywhere
   b. using the Internet to work from your home
   c. using video conferencing at your company

3. Who can benefit the most from digital identities?
   a. people who are poor
   b. people who are very poor
   c. people who are wealthy

B *Answer the following questions. Use complete and grammatically correct sentences.*

1. What is needed to telework?

2. What is some of the information stored on a digital identity card?

3. What is a very important use of a digital identity card?

C *The following statements have mistakes. Correct them.*

1. Governments are selling digital identity cards to their citizens.

2. The IC chip holds information about the cardholder.

3. In the future, the card will be able to be used like an international passport.

D *These sentences were used in the READING. Circle the word that has a similar meaning.*

1. The wages **tend** to be lower than those in urban areas.
   a. impossible　　b. improbable　　c. likely
2. The governments are **providing** their citizens with digital identities.
   a. depriving　　b. supplying　　c. withholding
3. As the name of the card **suggests**, it holds key information.
   a. conceals　　b. implies　　c. suppresses
4. The information contained by the card has been **verified**.
   a. authenticated　　b. contradicted　　c. denied

Listening

A *Listen to each question and circle the letter of the best answer.* 40

1. How much of the world's wealth is held by the richest 10%?
   a. 17%　　b. 70%　　c. 75%
2. ____?
   a. low income
   b. low and middle income
   c. middle income
3. ____?
   a. riding public transportation
   b. shopping
   c. voting

B *Listen and write the missing words.* 41

1. Since I got a better ______________, I can now telework.
2. The population in rural areas ______________ because young people are leaving.
3. A digital identity card __________ access to many __________ services.
4. Important ____________ information is ______________ on the IC chip.
5. ____.

Discussing

With a partner or in a small group, answer ONE of the following questions.

a. In the future, would you like to telework? Why or why not?
b. How do you protect your personal information?
c. What do you think of digital identity cards?

Take your notes in the space below:

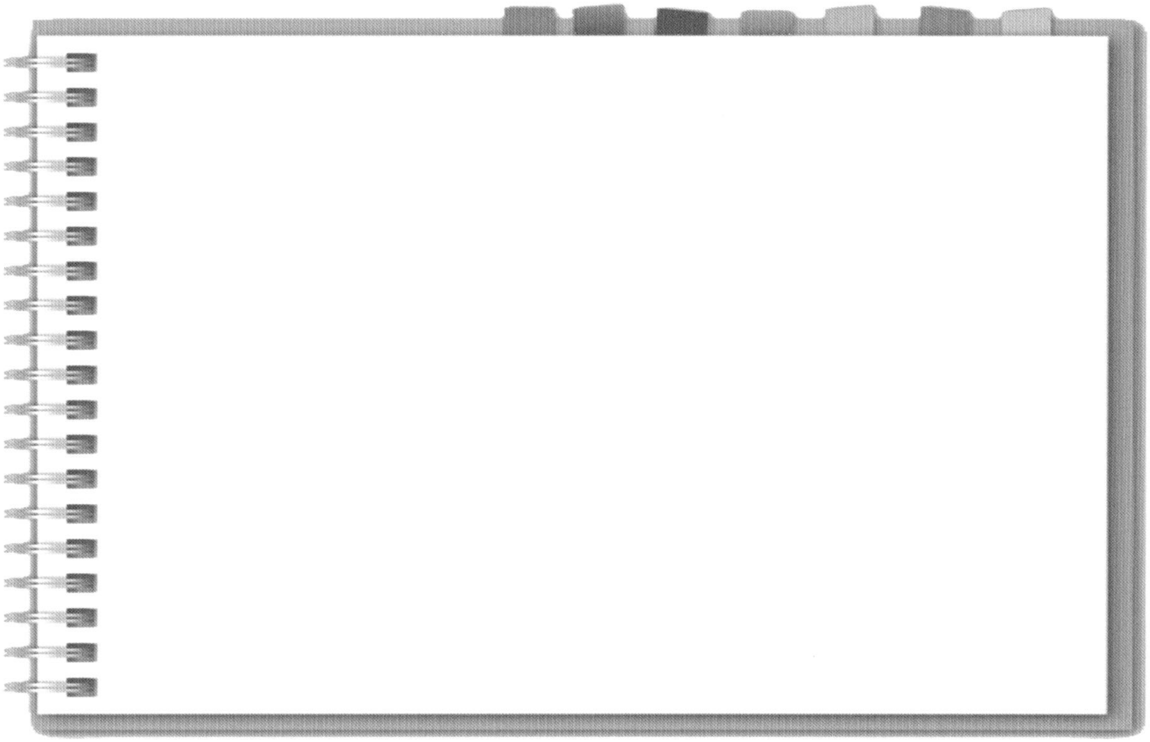

Sharing Information

Student A: Page 109
Student B: Page 121

Reviewing

Before you move on to the next unit, make sure you check all the boxes.

- ☐ I can describe income inequality.
- ☐ I can explain how digital identities can improve the lives of many people.
- ☐ I can list some of the ways that digital ID cards can be used.

13 Keeping Peace

At the end of this unit, you will ...

- ☐ understand how robots will change society.
- ☐ understand the dangers of robots in society.
- ☐ understand how robots will help us perform our jobs.

Vocabulary Focus

A *Match the words (1-12) with the correct definitions (a-l). The first one has been done for you!*

1.	(a)	affordable	7.	( )	enforcement
2.	( )	assembly	8.	( )	field
3.	( )	automated	9.	( )	leak
4.	( )	complex	10.	( )	pipelines
5.	( )	cybernetic	11.	( )	repetitive
6.	( )	deploy	12.	( )	suitable

a. something that we can buy without spending too much money
b. something that is right for a certain situation or purpose
c. something that works by itself
d. something that uses technology to work, like a robot or a computer
e. making sure people follow the rules
f. doing something over and over again
g. when something, like water or air, comes out of a hole or crack where it's not supposed to
h. an area of knowledge, a specific part
i. to make something happen, put something in place
j. the action of putting something together
k. long tubes that transport things from one place to another
l. something that is very difficult to understand or do

B *Complete the sentences with the words from MATCHING. You may need to change the word form.*

1. In the area of technology, robotics is one of the fast growing ____________.
2. The toys are made faster with the new ____________ line.
3. There was a ____________ in the roof and water was dripping onto the floor.
4. This jacket is ____________ for cold weather because it's warm and has a hood to protect your head.
5. Doing the same math problem over and over again can be very ____________ and boring.

C *Write two original sentences using words from MATCHING to help you remember them.*

1.
2.

Reading

Read this passage carefully and underline any unknown words.

Keeping Peace Around Us

Our way of life is evolving rapidly because of the advancements in technology. Robots are coming into our homes, offices, and hospitals to help us. Robotics is one of the fastest growing **fields** in science and technology. The main idea behind creating a robot is to **automate** some process or task that is currently carried out by humans. For example, robots can do **assembly** line work in factories. Although robots are not yet able to replace humans completely, they provide an excellent way to do things faster and more effectively.

The future is often described as "the age of robots," because robots will take over many human jobs and become a part of everyday life. However, this is a half truth because robots can be used for **repetitive** tasks but humans are still required for more **complex** ones. Robots can aid people by cleaning, carrying groceries, or preparing food, while others are being used to help people with physical limitations. Robots are used for the **automated** delivery of goods and to operate driverless vehicles.

Robots will perform jobs that are too challenging or not very **suitable** for humans. For example, robots can be used to inspect oil **pipelines** and search for **leaks** without endangering humans. In the next few years, we will see more and more robots in factories and mines. This is because robots are becoming more **affordable**, small enough to be transported by trucks and trains, and safe enough for humans to work alongside.

Robots are **deployed** to monitor borders around the world. Drones and unmanned vehicles with cameras and sensors patrol the air, land, and sea to detect and report any unusual or suspicious activity. Rapid response robots are used to detect hazardous materials and quickly contain and neutralize them. In emergency situations, search and rescue robots can be used to locate and free people from dangerous environments.

On the negative side, criminals may use robots to carry out crimes to avoid being discovered by the police. Robots can be physically controlled by people with cybernetic limbs, which enable them to perform intricate movements at superhuman speeds, or remotely by computer software. It is safe to say that in order to ensure that criminal activity is curbed, law **enforcement** must stay current with robotics developments.

379 words: ____ minutes ____ seconds

Understanding

A *Choose the best answer(s) to each question.*

1. What is the main idea behind creating a robot?
   a. To automate tasks currently done manually by humans
   b. To provide entertainment
   c. To replace all human jobs
2. What is one benefit of using robots for repetitive tasks?
   a. They are better at specialized tasks than humans.
   b. They are less expensive than hiring humans.
   c. They can perform tasks faster and more efficiently.
3. What is one area where robots are being used to perform tasks that are not suitable for humans?
   a. Cooking and cleaning
   b. Inspecting oil pipelines
   c. Serving food in restaurants

B *Answer the following questions. Use complete and grammatically correct sentences.*

1. How are robots changing the way we live our lives?

2. What are some examples of jobs that robots can do?

3. How are robots changing the job market?

C *The following statements have mistakes. Correct them.*

1. Robots will completely replace humans in all jobs.

2. The age of robots will mean that humans will lose their jobs.

3. Robots are always a good thing for society.

D *These sentences were used in the READING. Circle the word that has a similar meaning.*

1. Robots are used for **automated** delivery of goods and driverless cars.
   a. approximated   b. manual   c. mechanized
2. Robots can be controlled **remotely** by computer software
   a. directly   b. distantly   c. visually
3. Robots are **deployed** to monitor borders around the world.
   a. collected   b. dispatched   c. exploited
4. Robots are becoming more **affordable** and smaller.
   a. adorable   b. expensive   c. inexpensive

Listening

A *Listen to each question and circle the letter of the best answer.* 43

1. What is the main purpose of creating robots?
   a. To assist people with physical disabilities
   b. To commit criminal activities
   c. To do things faster and more efficiently than humans
2. ____?
   a. Because they are becoming more affordable and smaller
   b. Because they are becoming more expensive
   c. Because they are not safe for humans to work alongside them
3. ____?
   a. Robots can assist people with physical disabilities
   b. Robots can be used in criminal activities
   c. Robots can replace humans completely

B *Listen and write the missing words.* 44

1. The __________ of traffic laws is important for __________ public safety on roads.
2. __________ machines have __________ the need for manual __________ in many industries.
3. Oil __________ need to be __________ to prevent __________ and ensure the safe transportation of oil.
4. The ____________________ has made ____________________ more __________ for businesses.
5. ____.

Discussing

With a partner or in a small group, answer ONE of the following questions.

a. What are some ways that robots can help us?
b. Do you think it's a good idea to use robots to help police officers?
c. What would you like a robot to do to make your life easier?

Take your notes in the space below:

Sharing Information

Student A: Page 110
Student B: Page 122

Reviewing

Before you move on to the next unit, make sure you check all the boxes.

- ☐ I understand how robots will change society.
- ☐ I understand the dangers of robots in society.
- ☐ I understand how robots will help us performing our jobs.

14 Partnerships

At the end of this unit, you will ...

- ☐ understand how technology is helping us reach the SDGs.
- ☐ understand how lives can be improved in the future.
- ☐ understand how all the SDGs are interconnected.

Vocabulary Focus

A *Match the words (1-12) with the correct definitions (a-l). The first one has been done for you!*

1.	(d)	achieve	7.	( )	improvement
2.	( )	ambitious	8.	( )	innovation
3.	( )	decent	9.	( )	maintain
4.	( )	enforce	10.	( )	monitoring
5.	( )	flexible	11.	( )	occupation
6.	( )	impoverished	12.	( )	promote

a. to make sure a law or rule is followed
b. to keep in good condition by checking and repairing regularly
c. very poor
d. to do something successfully
e. having a strong desire to be powerful, rich, famous, etc.
f. watch and check something to make sure everything is okay
g. to help something to happen or develop
h. able to change to meet new situations or conditions
i. the job or role someone does
j. becoming better at something than you were before
k. good enough in quality
l. a new idea, method or device

B *Complete the sentences with the words from MATCHING. You may need to change the word form.*

1. The university student was looking for a(n) ______________ used car.
2. The ______________ country relied on international assistance during the crisis.
3. Although the machine was quite old, it was easy to ______________ it.
4. It seems like every few years there is a(n) ______________ that changes our lives.
5. The city is actively ______________ the use of public transportation with advertisements.

C *Write two original sentences using words from MATCHING to help you remember them. You may need to change the word form.*

1.
2.

Reading

45

Read this passage carefully and underline any unknown words.

Partnerships for the SDG Goals

It's no secret that we live in a world full of technology. In fact, it's hard to imagine a time when we didn't have access to smartphones, computers, or the Internet. In fact, technology is helping us make progress towards **achieving** the Sustainable Development Goals (SDGs). These **ambitious** goals aim to improve the lives of everyone, and tomorrow's technology will help us meet them.

Imagine a future where robots do all the dangerous jobs, like working in nuclear plants or operating heavy machinery. A world where widescale green energy generation reduces the impact that humans have on the environment. Also, access to technology means access to information, which is a huge step toward **achieving** our SDGs. With the Internet available everywhere we go on the planet, education is accessible to everyone, all the time. Also, publicly available information on a variety of topics such as self-care can help us all be healthier. In our world tomorrow, people can choose **occupations** and **flexible** jobs which allow parents to spend more time at home with their children while still **maintaining** a high standard of living. Finally, let's not forget about technology being used everywhere: devices that were once very expensive, such as water pumps and solar panels, are now affordable for even those living in **impoverished** regions. These technologies are providing people with clean water and electricity.

Looking more specifically at the 17 goals, **monitoring** technologies are helping us **maintain** our health and well-being (3 and 6), reduce food waste and empower communities with food monitoring (12). It has also helped us monitor climate change and address problems in the oceans and on the land (13, 14, 15). Advances in manufacturing have led to industry **innovation** and **improvements** in infrastructure (9). Education and information are more widely available so more people are able to find better jobs. Having access to decent work helps people escape from poverty and hunger, and in turn reduces inequalities (1, 2, 4, 8 and 10). Access to information also means that people can find forums where gender, race and many other issues can be discussed and awareness can be raised (5). Technology can provide **affordable** and clean energy, allowing communities all over the world to meet their energy needs (7 and 11). Lastly, advances in software and hardware allow law **enforcement** and governments to **enforce** justice and secure our cities (16).

Where is SDG 17 you ask? Well, this is it. We are all now working together to achieve the other 16 goals which means that we are creating a sustainable model that helps develop ways to measure and **promote** the sustainable development of our world tomorrow.

441 words: ____ minutes ____ seconds

Understanding

A *Choose the best answer(s) to each question.*

1. How can technology help us achieve the Sustainable Development Goals (SDGs)?
   a. By creating robots that can replace human workers
   b. By making smartphones and computers available to everyone
   c. By providing access to information and improving our lives
2. What are some examples of how technology is helping us achieve the SDGs?
   a. Creating more dangerous jobs for humans to do
   b. Making devices like solar panels and water pumps more expensive
   c. Providing access to education, clean water, and electricity
3. Which SDG is being achieved by working towards the other 16 goals?
   a. SDG 15　　b. SDG 16　　c. SDG 17

B *Answer the following questions. Use complete and grammatically correct sentences.*

1. What are some examples of how technology is helping us achieve the Sustainable Development Goals (SDGs)?

2. How does access to technology help reduce inequalities?

3. How is technology being used to promote justice and secure cities?

C *The following statements have mistakes. Correct them.*

1. The SDGs will be achieved through technology.

2. Technology can solve all of our problems related to poverty, hunger, and inequality.

3. SDG 17 is the most important goal because it brings all of the other goals together.

D *These sentences were used in the READING. Circle the word that has a similar meaning.*

1. These **ambitious** goals aim to improve the lives of everyone.
   a. aspiring b. easy c. satisfying
2. Imagine a future where robots do all the **dangerous** jobs.
   a. demanding b. hazardous c. wholesome
3. Monitoring technologies are helping us **maintain** our health and well-being.
   a. abandon b. neglect c. sustain
4. Technology can provide **affordable** and clean energy.
   a. affluent b. expensive c. inexpensive

Listening

A *Listen to each question and circle the letter of the best answer.* 46

1. What are the Sustainable Development Goals (SDGs)?
   a. Goals to create robots that can do all jobs
   b. Goals to improve the lives of everyone
   c. Goals to promote technology advancement
2. ____?
   a. By making people spend more time at work
   b. By reducing access to education and information
   c. By reducing the impact humans have on the environment
3. ____?
   a. Allowing communities to meet their energy needs
   b. Creating more dangerous jobs for humans
   c. Providing access to clean water and electricity

B *Listen and write the missing words.* 47

1. Monitoring your daily steps with a ____________ is a great way to stay ______________.
2. ______________ allows employees to ______________ and __________ lives.
3. With _________ and _________, anyone can ________________.
4. Regular __________ of your car's __________ can help ______________ ______________.
5. ____ ______________________.

Discussing

With a partner or in a small group, answer ONE of the following questions.

a. What does it mean to work in partnership for the SDG goals?
b. Why is it important for countries to work together to achieve the SDG goals?
c. Can you think of ways you can work with others to help achieve the SDG goals?

Take your notes in the space below:

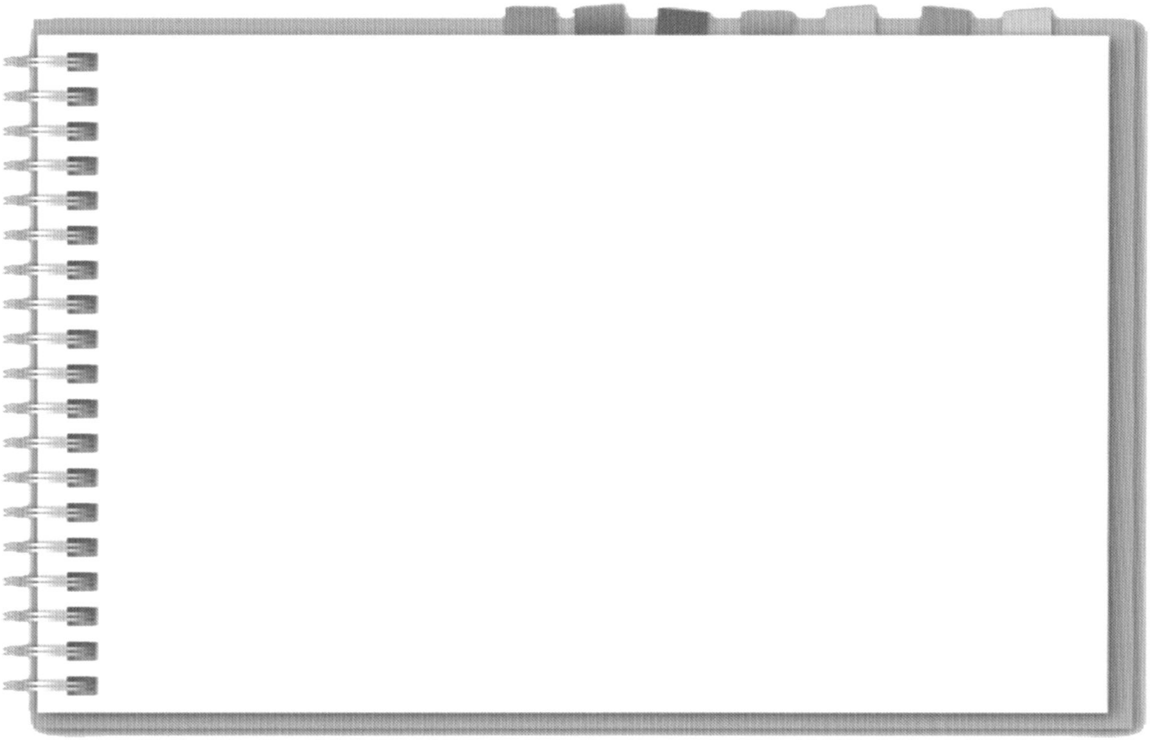

Sharing Information

Student A: Page 111
Student B: Page 123

Reviewing

Before you move on to the next unit, make sure you check all the boxes.

☐ I understand how technology is helping us reach the SDGs.
☐ I understand how lives can be improved in the future.
☐ I understand how all the SDGs are interconnected.

15 Review: Units 11-14

Part 1 Photographs

48

You will hear three short statements. Look at the picture and choose the statement that best describes what you see in the picture.

1.

Ⓐ Ⓑ Ⓒ

2.

Ⓐ Ⓑ Ⓒ

3.

Ⓐ Ⓑ Ⓒ

4.

Ⓐ Ⓑ Ⓒ

Part 2 Question-Response

49

You will hear a question or statement followed by three responses. Choose the best response.

1. Mark your answer. Ⓐ Ⓑ Ⓒ
2. Mark your answer. Ⓐ Ⓑ Ⓒ
3. Mark your answer. Ⓐ Ⓑ Ⓒ
4. Mark your answer. Ⓐ Ⓑ Ⓒ
5. Mark your answer. Ⓐ Ⓑ Ⓒ
6. Mark your answer. Ⓐ Ⓑ Ⓒ

Part 3 Short Conversations

50

You will hear short conversations between two people. Choose the best answer to each of the three questions.

Dialogue 1

1. Who are the speakers?
   A. Classmates B. Friends
   C. Neighbors
   (A) (B) (C)

2. What is the man's main concern?
   A. About privacy issues B. About suspicious behavior
   C. About the benefits of robots
   (A) (B) (C)

3. What is the man going to do after jogging?
   A. Check his doorstep B. Look at the newspaper
   C. Patrol the streets
   (A) (B) (C)

Dialogue 2

1. Who are the speakers?
   A. Colleagues B. Friends
   C. Strangers
   (A) (B) (C)

2. What are they talking about?
   A. Changing office buildings B. Connecting to the Wi-Fi
   C. Looking for a Wi-Fi connection
   (A) (B) (C)

3. What is the man likely to do next?
   A. Get more information B. Go to the other building
   C. Try the other Wi-Fi network
   (A) (B) (C)

Part 4 Short Talk

51

You will hear a short talk. Choose the best answer to each of the three questions.

1. Who is likely the speaker?
   A. A company manager B. A government official
   C. A school principal D. An entrepreneur
   (A) (B) (C) (D)

2. Which is a skill required by the jobs of the future?
   A. Critical thinking B. Ones that are in high demand today
   C. State-of-the-art technology D. Web development
   (A) (B) (C) (D)

3. Why was this program launched?
   A. To encourage students to take advantage of it
   B. To help students pass their classes
   C. To teach students about the World Economic Forum
   D. To teach students necessary skills for their future jobs
   (A) (B) (C) (D)

Part 5 Text Completion

Four words or phrases are missing in the text. Choose the best answers to complete the text.

Technology has played a significant role in revolutionizing the field of education. With the advent of online (1) platforms, educational apps, and other digital tools, education has become more accessible and affordable than ever before. Technology has helped to (2) educational inequalities by making learning resources available to a wider audience.

For example, students in remote areas can now access high-quality educational materials through online platforms, which was not possible before. Technology has also made it possible for students with (3) to access educational resources and participate in learning activities with their peers. Additionally, digital tools have enabled teachers to personalize learning experiences for students, making sure they address students' needs and abilities.

Overall, technology has the potential to reduce educational inequalities and provide (4) opportunities to all students, regardless of their background or location. By doing so, it can contribute to creating a better society, where everyone has a chance to realize their potential and lead fulfilling lives.

1. A. gaming B. learning
   C. market D. payment
   (A) (B) (C) (D)

2. A. reduce B. refuse
   C. release D. reuse
   (A) (B) (C) (D)

3. A. disabilities B. high IQ
   C. hunger D. inequalities
   (A) (B) (C) (D)

4. A. biased B. dissimilar
   C. equal D. varying
   (A) (B) (C) (D)

Part 6 Reading Comprehension

Read the following text. Choose the best answer to each question.

Discover How Technology is Making Our Community Safer!

Come and join us for a day of excitement and innovation as we showcase the latest technology being used by our local police officers to fight crime and keep our community safe. Witness a live demonstration of a remote-controlled robot that can disarm bombs and explosives, eliminating the risk of harm to our brave officers. Our knowledgeable officers will explain how technology is changing the way they work and how it's making our community a safer place to live. Enjoy live music from Generations, a popular local band, free refreshments, and the chance to meet and greet our officers. Don't miss out on this unique opportunity to learn about the cutting-edge tools being used to protect our community.

Place: In front of Town Hall (April 4)

Introduction (10:00 AM - 10:10 AM)
Welcome speech by Captain Holt and a brief overview of the event and what attendees can expect to see

Technology Showcase (10:10 AM - 10:40 AM)
Local police officers showcase new technology used to combat crime
Explanation of how these tools are making our community safer
Interactive demos of some of the tools, including simulations of real-life situations

Live Demonstration (10:40 AM - 11:20 PM)
The highlight of the event. Watch how a robot can disarm bombs remotely
Explanation of this technology and how it can help protect our police officers and community
Q&A session with the officers in charge of the robot

Meet and Greet (11:20 PM - 12:00 PM)
Opportunity for attendees to meet and talk to the police officers who showcased the technology
Take photos and ask questions about their work

Free event. For inquiries, please call 903-825-TALK (7611).

1. Where is this text likely to be found?
   A. A business magazine　　B. A local newspaper
   C. An encyclopedia
   Ⓐ Ⓑ Ⓒ

2. Who is this event intended for?
   A. Children and teenagers　　B. Scientists and experts
   C. The general public
   Ⓐ Ⓑ Ⓒ

3. What is true about the event?
   A. There will be a Q&A session with the robot designer.
   B. Officers will be learning about the technology.
   C. Officers will be greeting the attendees.

Ⓐ Ⓑ Ⓒ

4. How can people attend the event?
   A. By going to the Town Hall on April 10
   B. By watching it live
   C. People need to call in advance

Ⓐ Ⓑ Ⓒ

Part 7 Case Study

52

Scenario: Marei City is a bustling metropolis with a population of over 5 million people. Despite its vibrant economy and cultural attractions, the city has long struggled with high crime rates, particularly in its downtown area. The police department has tried various strategies to address this issue, but the crime rate has remained stubbornly high.

A small group of lawmakers are discussing crime at a Town Hall meeting. What are some of their ideas to deal with the issue?

Listen to their conversation and take notes in the space below.

The lawmakers have proposed these implementation steps to the mayor of Marei City:

Implementation idea 1
Develop a comprehensive plan for robot deployment: The city should conduct a thorough assessment of its crime hotspots and determine where the robots will be most effective. The deployment plan should include the number of robots needed, their locations, and their patrol routes.

Implementation idea 2
Train police officers on how to use the robot patrolling system: The success of the robot patrolling system depends on the police officers who will be monitoring the robots. It's essential to provide them with adequate training on how to use the system and interpret the data that the robots collect.

Implementation idea 3
Conduct public awareness campaigns: It's important to educate the public about the robot patrolling system and its benefits. This can be done through public awareness campaigns, community meetings, and other outreach efforts. The public should understand how the robots will be used and the steps taken to protect their privacy.

Implementation idea 4
Establish partnerships with local businesses: Local businesses can be valuable partners in the implementation of the robot patrolling system. They can provide support by allowing the robots to patrol their premises, sharing video footage of criminal activity, and providing feedback on the system's effectiveness.

Implementation idea 5
Conduct regular evaluations: The effectiveness of the robot patrolling system should be evaluated regularly to determine its impact on crime rates. This can be done by analyzing crime statistics, conducting surveys of residents and business owners, and gathering feedback from police officers. The results of the evaluations can be used to fine-tune the deployment of the robots and make improvements to the system over time.

All of these implementation ideas have advantages and disadvantages that need to be considered when choosing the best course of action for Marei City. Choose ONE of the solutions and take notes.

With the members of your group, discuss each of the initiatives using your notes. Together, choose TWO initiatives for Marei City.

Sharing Information: Student A

Unit 1 *Student A*

a. Read this short passage about SDGs to your partner.

The SDGs were created by the United Nations to address some of the world's most urgent issues, such as poverty, inequality, and climate change. The 17 goals are all connected to each other, meaning that progress in one goal can support progress in others. For example, improving access to education and empowering women can have a positive impact on reducing poverty and inequality. Each goal has specific targets and clear explanations, so it is possible to track progress over time. It is important to remember that the SDGs are not the responsibility of just a few governments, but everyone, including you and me. Everyone has a role to play and we should all work together to achieve the SDGs by 2030. (121 words)

b. Ask these three questions to your partner.

1. What are the SDGs and why were they created?

2. How are the SDGs interconnected?

3. Who is responsible for achieving the SDGs?

c. Your partner will read about MDGs. Listen carefully.

d. Answer these three questions.

1. What were the Millennium Development Goals (MDGs)?

2. What was one of the achievements of the MDGs?

3. What is the connection between the MDGs and the SDGs?

Unit 2 *Student A*

With a partner, complete this chart.

Device Name	Health Features	Exercise Features	Smart Features	Design Features	Cost
Fit Watch	steps taken		call notifications		$300
		15 workout modes		water resistant to 50m	
	sleep tracking		music		
Life Watch		6 workout modes		40 mm screen	
	calories burned		text notifications		
		pace and distance *		5-day battery life	
Victory 5	steps taken		call notifications		$150
		swim tracking		waterproof	
	floors climbed		app notifications		
Excite PB		6 workout modes		38 mm by 15 mm	
	guided breathing		text notifications		
		pace and distance *		5-day battery life	
FrontRunner	steps taken		apps		$350
		12 workout modes		full-color display	
	floors climbed		built-in GPS		
SmartWatch		reminders to move		45 mm screen	
	sleep tracking		music		
		pace and distance		3 buttons	

*requires smartphone

Useful phrases

"What is a health feature of the Fit Watch?"

"What does resistant mean?"

"How do you spell resistant?"

"How do you say resistant in Japanese?"

a. Read part 1 of a story about a boy named Marcos to your partner.

Marcos was just a boy, but he had to grow up quickly. His father had passed away a long time ago, leaving him with his mother, grandmother, and sister. Despite his young age, he knew that he had to do something to help his family escape poverty. During the day, Marcos would gather garbage from the streets and alleys around his neighborhood. He would separate the recyclable materials from the trash and sell them to recycling centers for a small amount of money. Although it was not much, the money he earned helped his family put food on the table. At night, Marcos would attend classes run by volunteers who came to his community. They taught him and other children how to read and write. Marcos loved learning, and he knew that education was the key to a better future. Despite the challenges, Marcos never gave up. With his hard work and perseverance, Marcos was slowly but surely making a difference in his family's life. (165 words)

b. Ask these three questions to your partner.

1. How does Marcos try to earn money to support his family?
2. Who helps Marcos with his studies at night?
3. How does the poverty cycle impact Marcos and his family?

c. Your partner will read part 2 of the story about Marcos. Listen carefully.

d. Answer these three questions.

1. What did Marcos do to improve his situation?
2. What was his ultimate goal?
3. How does education play a role in Marcos' journey to break the poverty cycle?

Unit 4 *Student A*

With a partner, complete this chart.

Product	Amount of Water (in liters)	Green Water	Blue Water	Grey Water	Solution
1 cup of coffee (125 ml)	132		1%		Switch to tea (27 litres / 250 ml cup)
1 kilogram of white rice		68%		11%	
1 kilogram of beef	15,415		4%		Switch to chicken (4,325 litres / kilogram)
1 kilogram of mangoes or guava		73%		7%	
1 glass of wine (125 ml)	109		16%	14%	Switch to barley beer (74 litres for 250 ml glass)
1 kilogram of sugar (from sugar cane)		66%		6%	
1 banana (200 grams)	160		12%		Switch to apples (125 litres / apple)
1 kilogram of corn (maize)		77%		16%	

Essential Knowledge

Blue Water: Surface water and groundwater required (evaporated or used directly) to produce an item.

Green Water: Rainwater required (evaporated or used directly) to make an item.

Grey Water: Freshwater required to dilute the wastewater generated in manufacturing, in order to maintain water quality (defined by local regulations)

Useful phrases

How much water is used to produce a cup of coffee?

What percentage of green water is used?

How do you spell maize?

How do you say maize in Japanese?

Unit 6 *Student A*

a. Read this short passage about the Ugly Food Movement to your partner.

"Ugly" foods are fruits and vegetables that people do not want to buy because of their look. Farmers, supermarkets, and restaurants often throw them away because customers do not want them. Worried about the high levels of food waste in Europe, the European Union announced the "European Year Against Food Waste" in 2014. The third largest supermarket chain in France started a promotion to encourage customers to buy "ugly food" instead. Some of the stars of the unattractive fruits and vegetables were: the ugly carrot, the ridiculous potato, and the grotesque apple. These ugly fruits and vegetables were offered for 30% less than the "beautiful foods." At first, the customers were not interested in buying them. The supermarket started making soups and juices for them to try. The customers were convinced and began buying all of these unwanted fruits and vegetables. (141 words)

b. Ask these three questions to your partner.

1. What did the European Union do in 2014?

2. What were some of the "stars" of the supermarket's promotion?

3. How did the supermarket convince customers to buy ugly foods?

c. Your partner will read about indoor composting. Listen carefully.

d. Answer these three questions.

1. What things do you need for a kitchen composter?

2. What are good things to compost?

3. Why shouldn't you add things like melons?

Unit 7 *Student A*

With a partner, complete this chart.

Smart Technology	Impact 1	Impact 2	Impact 3
Smart Transportation	Reduces traffic congestion		Reduces greenhouse gas emissions
Public transportation systems (Powered by clean energy)		Reduces greenhouse gas emissions	
Smart Waste Management	Improves waste collection and recycling processes		Generates renewable energy from waste
Green roofs		Reduce heat island effect	
Urban parks and green spaces	Provides recreational opportunities		Reduces urban heat island effect
Vertical farms		Reduces transportation emissions	

Useful phrases

"What is the first/second/third impact of smart transportation?

"What does emissions mean?"

"How do you spell emissions?"

"How do you say emissions in Japanese?"

Unit 8 *Student A*

a. Read this short passage about wind energy to your partner.

In 2019, around 2% of all electricity generated in the world came from wind. This number is expected to increase as more countries around the world have started to invest in wind generated electricity. Even though the amount of investment has been different from country to country, we have seen a steady increase in the "installed wind capacity" (measured in Gigawatts, or GW), meaning that countries are installing more equipment that can generate energy from wind. As an example, from 2010 to 2020, Japan went from 2.29 GW to 4.37 GW, almost doubling it. However, Japan's installed wind capacity is quite low when compared to the United States of America, a country that almost tripled its installed wind capacity going from 39.13 GW to 118.63 GW in the same period. (134 words)

b. Ask these three questions to your partner.

1. In 2019, how much of the world energy was generated from wind?
2. How do we know that countries have started to invest in electricity generation from wind?
3. How does Japan's installed wind capacity compare to that of the United States of America?

c. Your partner will read about batteries. Listen carefully.

d. Answer these three questions.

1. What are three things that scientists have to think about?
2. The latest batteries can store much more energy. How much more?
3. Why are batteries important for your future?

Unit 9 *Student A*

a. Read this short passage about remote work to your partner.

Remote work, also known as telecommuting, has become increasingly popular in recent years. It refers to working from a location other than a traditional office, such as from home or a co-working space. Among the benefits of remote work is the fact that remote work offers greater flexibility. Employees can set their own schedules and work at times that suit them best. This allows individuals to better balance their work and personal lives, which can lead to increased productivity and job satisfaction. Remote work can also lead to cost savings for both employers and employees. Employers can save money on office space and equipment, while employees can save on transportation and other work-related expenses. In addition, remote work can also benefit the environment by reducing commuting and lowering carbon emissions. (130 words)

b. Ask these three questions to your partner.

1. What is telecommuting?
2. What are some benefits of remote work?
3. Why is remote work good for the environment?

c. Your partner will read part 2 about remote work. Listen carefully.

d. Answer these three questions.

1. What is a problem with remote work?
2. How can remote work be bad for mental health?
3. What are some technical challenges that can come with remote work?

Unit 11 *Student A*

a. Read this short passage about floating schools to your partner.

During the monsoon season in Bangladesh, which runs from June to October, approximately 80% of the annual rainfall occurs. By the end of the season, more than ⅓ of the country is underwater with many roads being unusable and up to 4,000 schools are closed. One man, Mohammed Rezwan, had a clever solution. He said, "if the children cannot come to school because of floods, then the school should go to them by boat." In 2002, he started a nonprofit organization and built the first school boat. Since then, they have been able to build more than 25 of these boats and help over 80,000 students. These traditional Bangladeshi boats, called Noka, have been modified with weatherproof windows, solar panels, and metal beams. Each boat has a laptop, library and room for 30 to 35 students. Students learn basic literacy and essential life skills. Classes are also held for adults to help them become better farmers. (158 words)

* monsoon 季節風

b. Ask these three questions to your partner.

1. When is the monsoon season in Bangladesh?
2. How have the traditional boats been modified?
3. What do the students learn?

c. Your partner will read about educational robots. Listen carefully.

d. Answer these three questions.

1. What are researchers developing?
2. Who are the intended users of QTrobot?
3. What can the robot recognize?

Unit 12 *Student A*

With a partner, complete this chart.

Country	No ID	ID	Digital ID	Card Name	Information
Bangladesh		83 million		National Identity Card	
India	162 million		257 million		Name, DOB, sex, address, ID number, fingerprints, photo, iris scan, QR code
Indonesia		96 million		e-KTP (Electronic Identity Card)	
Nigeria	141 million		20 million		Name, DOB, sex, height, nationality, photo, signature, fingerprints, address, identity number
Pakistan		89 million		Smart National Identity Card	

*DOB = date of birth
A digital trail (or footprint) is a record of your activities.

Useful phrases

"How many people in India have a digital ID?"
"What does DOB mean?"
"How do you spell signature?"
"How do you say signature in Japanese?"

Unit 13 *Student A*

a. Read about technology to your partner.

Technology plays a crucial role in maintaining peace and stability in the world. One of the most important ways technology helps to keep peace is through communication. Advances in communication technology have made it easier for people all over the world to connect with one another and share information quickly and easily. This has enabled governments, international organizations, and individuals to work together more effectively to prevent conflicts and promote peace. Another way technology helps to keep peace is through surveillance and monitoring. With the help of advanced technologies such as drones, satellites, and cameras, it is possible to monitor and track potential problems before they become too big to deal with. This allows governments and international organizations to take action before small problems become big problems and prevent violence and protect the safety of civilians. (136 words)

b. Ask these three questions to your partner.

1. How does technology help in maintaining peace and stability in the world?
2. How have advances in communication technology made it easier for people to work together to prevent conflicts and promote peace?
3. What is surveillance technology and how has it helped maintain peace?

c. Your partner will read part 2 about technology. Listen carefully.

d. Answer these three questions.

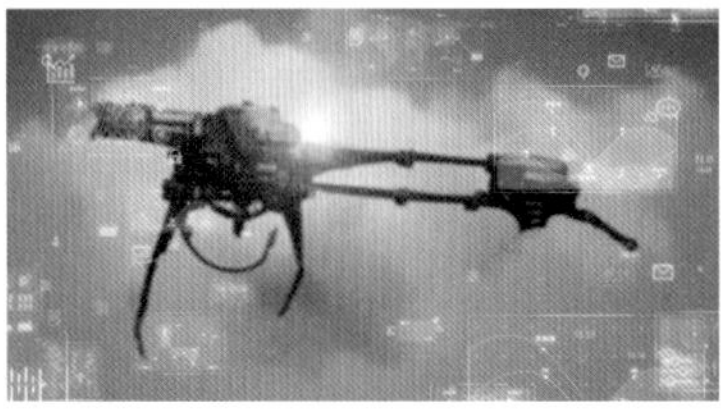

1. What is the role of advanced technologies in peacekeeping missions?
2. How have defensive technologies been used to help maintain peace?
3. What is the benefit of using technology in peacekeeping missions?

Unit 14 *Student A*

With a partner, complete this chart.

SDG	Goal	Action 1	Action 2
1		Donating food to people in need.	
2	Zero Hunger		Buying locally grown food.
3		Encouraging exercise.	
4	Quality Education		Volunteering at a local school
5		Promoting women's rights.	
6	Clean Water and Sanitation		Conserving water.
7		Switching to renewable energy sources like solar and wind power.	
8	Decent Work and Economic Growth		Buying locally made products.
9		Encouraging the use of new technologies and sustainable infrastructure.	

Useful phrases

"What is the goal of SDG 1?"

"What is an action of SDG 1?"

"If we donate food to people in need, which SDG are we helping?

"How do you spell encouraging?"

"How do you say conserving in Japanese?"

Sharing Information: Student B

Unit 1 *Student B*

a. Your partner will read about SDGs. Listen carefully.

b. Answer these three questions.

1. What are the SDGs and why were they created?
2. How are the SDGs interconnected?
3. Who is responsible for achieving the SDGs?

c. Read this short passage about MDGs to your partner.

The MDGs were a set of global development goals aimed at reducing poverty and promoting sustainable development. The eight goals were agreed upon by world leaders and the United Nations in 2000 and set a deadline of 2015 for their achievement. One of the greatest achievements of the MDGs was the drop in the number of children out of school by almost half, from 100 million in 2000 to 57 million in 2015. With more kids in school, especially girls, also helped to promote gender equality. The MDGs also helped to increase access to clean water, reduce child mortality, and improve maternal health. Although not all of the goals were fully achieved, the MDGs set the foundation for continued progress and the development of the SDGs. (126 words)

d. Ask these three questions to your partner.

1. What were the Millennium Development Goals (MDGs)?
2. What was one of the achievements of the MDGs?
3. What is the connection between the MDGs and the SDGs?

Unit 2 *Student B*

With a partner, complete this chart.

Device Name	Health Features	Exercise Features	Smart Features	Design Features	Cost
Fit Watch		heart rate monitor		45 mm screen	
	calories burned		apps		
		pace and distance		7-day battery life	
Life Watch	steps taken		call notifications		$200
		reminders to move		full-color display	
	sleep tracking		music *		
Victory 5		6 workout modes		37mm screen	
	calories burned		text notifications		
		goal setting		20-day battery life	
Excite PB	steps taken		call notifications		
		goal setting		black & white display	$100
	sleep tracking		app notifications		
FrontRunner		heart rate monitor		40 mm screen	
	sleep tracking		music		
		running coach		7-day battery life	
SmartWatch	steps taken		mobile payments		$300
		6 workout modes		full-color display	
	floors climbed		built-in GPS		

*requires smartphone

Useful phrases

"What is a health feature of the Fit Watch?"
"What does waterproof mean?"
"How do you spell waterproof?"
"How do you say waterproof in Japanese?"

Unit 3 *Student B*

a. Your partner will read part 1 of a story about a boy named Marcos. Listen carefully.

b. Answer these three questions.

1. How does Marcos try to earn money to support his family?
2. Who helps Marcos with his studies at night?
3. How does the poverty cycle impact Marcos and his family?

c. Read part 2 of the story about Marcos to your partner.

Marcos was determined to escape poverty. He knew the importance of education, so he studied hard every night to improve his reading, writing, and math skills. With the help of volunteers, Marcos was able to gain the knowledge and confidence he needed to apply for better jobs. At first, Marcos struggled to find work, but he refused to give up. He continued to study until he finally got a job that paid enough to support his family. With his economic stability, Marcos began to give back to his community, by volunteering at local schools and youth centers. As Marcos advanced in his career, he made even more money. He never forgot where he came from, and he always made time to give back to the people who had helped him along the way. Thanks to his hard work and determination, Marcos was able to break the cycle of poverty for himself and his family, and he became an inspiration to others. (161 words)

d. Ask these three questions to your partner.

1. What did Marcos do to improve his situation?
2. What was his ultimate goal?
3. How does education play a role in Marcos' journey to break the poverty cycle?

Unit 4 *Student B*

With a partner, complete this chart.

Product	Amount of Water (in liters)	Green Water	Blue Water	Grey Water	Solution
1 cup of coffee (125 ml)		96%		3%	
1 kilogram of white rice	2,497		20%		Switch to pasta (1,849 litres / kilogram)
1 kilogram of beef		94%		3%	
1 kilogram of mangoes or guava	1,800		20%		Switch to oranges (560 litres)
1 glass of wine (125 ml)		70%		14%	
1 kilogram of sugar (from sugar cane)	1,782		27%		Switch to sugar from sugar beet (920 litres / kilogram)
1 banana (200 grams)		84%		4%	
1 kilogram of corn (maize)	1,222		7%		Switch to potatoes (287 litres / kilogram)

Essential Knowledge

Blue Water: Surface water and groundwater required (evaporated or used directly) to produce an item.

Green Water: Rainwater required (evaporated or used directly) to make an item.

Grey Water: Freshwater required to dilute the wastewater generated in manufacturing, in order to maintain water quality (defined by local regulations)

Useful phrases

How much water is used to produce a cup of coffee?

What percentage of green water is used?

How do you spell maize?

How do you say maize in Japanese?

Unit 6 *Student B*

a. Your partner will read about the Ugly Food Movement. Listen carefully.

b. Answer these three questions.

1. What did the European Union do in 2014?
2. What were some of the "stars" of the supermarket's promotion?
3. How did the supermarket convince customers to buy ugly foods?

c. Read this short passage about indoor composting to your partner.

A kitchen composter is easy to set up and use. A plastic storage container with a lid, shredded newspaper, and some dirt is all you need. You can put almost all food scraps in an outdoor composter, but with an indoor one you have to be a bit more careful because of the smells. The best things are fruit and vegetable scraps, egg shells, coffee grounds, and tea bags. Never put cooked food, meat, dairy products, or fish bones in it. Also, it is best to avoid smelly things like onion peels and watery scraps such as melons. When you add to your composter, add a handful of shredded paper or dry leaves to make sure it isn't too wet. If it is too wet it will smell bad and attract flies! The last thing that you need to do is mix the bin every three or four days so the composter works efficiently. (154 words)

d. Ask these three questions to your partner.

1. What things do you need for a kitchen composter?
2. What are good things to compost?
3. Why shouldn't you add things like melons?

Unit 7 *Student B*

With a partner, complete this chart.

Smart Technology	Impact 1	Impact 2	Impact 3
Smart Transportation		Reduces air pollution	
Public transportation systems (Powered by clean energy)	Reduces air pollution		Provides convenient and cost-effective transportation
Smart Waste Management		Reduces landfill waste	
Green roofs	Absorbs rainwater		Improves air quality
Urban parks and green spaces		Improves mental and physical health	
Vertical farms	Maximizes food production in urban areas		Reduces water usage

Useful phrases

"What is the first/second/third impact of smart transportation?

"What does emissions mean?"

"How do you spell emissions?"

"How do you say emissions in Japanese?"

Unit 8 *Student B*

a. Your partner will read about wind energy. Listen carefully.

b. Answer these three questions.

1. In 2019, how much of the world energy was generated from wind?
2. How do we know that countries have started to invest in electricity generation from wind?
3. How does Japan's installed wind capacity compare to that of the United States of America?

c. Your partner will read about batteries. Listen carefully.

When people talk about technology it is easy to think about smartphones or robots. Many people forget about a very important component that makes most technology around us possible: batteries. There is a lot of technology inside a battery and a lot of research is being done by scientists. It is not only necessary to think about the energy that will be created, but also about the elements and metals that will be used in a battery. In the last fifty years, the amount of energy stored by batteries has increased more than four times. In other words, it is like your 12-hour smartphone would be usable for only 3 hours if it were using batteries made fifty years ago. With the world moving towards electric cars and smart cities, batteries are surely going to play a very important role in the future. (143 words)

d. Ask these three questions to your partner.

1. What are three things that scientists have to think about?
2. The latest batteries can store much more energy. How much more?
3. Why are batteries important for your future?

Unit 9 *Student B*

a. Your partner will read about remote work. Listen carefully.

b. Answer these three questions.

1. What is telecommuting?
2. What are some benefits of remote work?
3. Why is remote work good for the environment?

c. Read part 2 about remote work to your partner.

Remote work has many benefits, but it also comes with some challenges. One of the problems with remote work is that it can be isolating. Without face-to-face interaction with colleagues, employees may feel lonely or disconnected from their team. This can lead to decreased motivation and job satisfaction. Remote work can also blur the boundaries between work and personal life. While some employees can successfully manage their time and find the right balance between personal and work life, without a clear separation between the two, it can be difficult for many employees to disconnect and recharge. This can lead to burnout and other negative effects on mental health. In addition, remote work can also present technical challenges. Employees may encounter issues with their internet connection or computer hardware, which can disrupt their workflow and productivity. (135 words)

d. Ask these three questions to your partner.

1. What is a problem with remote work?
2. How can remote work be bad for mental health?
3. What are some technical challenges that can come with remote work?

Unit 11 *Student B*

a. Your partner will read about floating schools. Listen carefully.

b. Answer these three questions.

1. When is the monsoon season in Bangladesh?
2. How have the traditional boats been modified?
3. What do the students learn?

c. Read this short passage about educational robots to your partner.

Because of advances in artificial intelligence, robots are becoming more widely used. Unlike industrial robots used in factories, social robots are made to directly interact with people. Researchers around the world are developing robots to help teach social and education skills to students with physical and learning disabilities. One company has developed the QTrobot, a 64 cm. tall humanoid robot that teaches social and communication skills to children with autism. Many children with autism have difficulty with conversation so there are lessons such as: asking and responding to questions, and how to start and finish conversations. The robot uses simple expressions and exaggerated gestures to help the child understand easily. Also, because the QTrobot can recognize the emotions and poses of the child and respond in a consistent and predictable way, it helps the child relax. The robot can repeat the same expressions and movements exactly the same way without becoming tired or frustrated. This helps the child practice and master new skills. (163 words)

* autism 自閉症

d. Ask these three questions to your partner.

1. What are researchers developing?
2. Who are the intended users of QTrobot?
3. What can the robot recognize?

Unit 12 *Student B*

With a partner, complete this chart.

Country	No ID	ID	Digital ID	Card Name	Information
Bangladesh	53 million		30 million		Name, parents' names, DOB, ID number, photo, fingerprints
India		935 million		Aadhaar (means foundation or base)	
Indonesia	21 million		150 million		Name, DOB, religion, occupation, address, marital status, photo, signature, fingerprints, contactless tech
Nigeria		35 million		e-ID (National Electronic Identification Card)	
Pakistan	76 million		36 million		Name, father's name, gender, DOB, photo, address, signature, identity number

*DOB = date of birth
A digital trail (or footprint) is a record of your activities.

■ Useful phrases

"How many people in India have a digital ID?"
"What does DOB mean?"
"How do you spell signature?"
"How do you say signature in Japanese?"

Unit 13 *Student B*

a. Your partner will read about technology. Listen carefully.

b. Answer these three questions.

1. How does technology help in maintaining peace and stability in the world?
2. How have advances in communication technology made it easier for people to work together to prevent conflicts and promote peace?
3. What is surveillance technology and how has it helped maintain peace?

c. Read part 2 about technology to your partner.

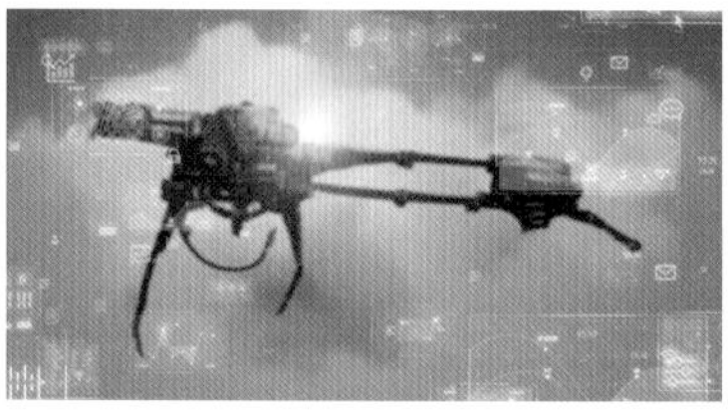

Advanced technology plays a critical role in peacekeeping missions worldwide, providing military personnel with advanced communication, surveillance, and defensive technologies to navigate dangerous environments and protect civilians. These technologies help reduce casualties and prevent conflicts from escalating. Communication technologies also enable quick responses to threats, while surveillance technologies, such as drones and satellites, monitor potential threats and prevent conflicts from escalating. Additionally, defensive technologies like armor and ballistic shields protect military personnel during peacekeeping missions. Another way technology has been used is through aid during times of conflict by efficiently identifying areas that need assistance and providing medical assistance to injured people. Governments, international organizations and individuals are all able to work together more effectively to promote peace and prevent conflicts. It is clear that technology has become an important tool in maintaining peace and stability worldwide. (137 words)

d. Ask these three questions to your partner.

1. What is the role of advanced technologies in peacekeeping missions?
2. How have defensive technologies been used to help maintain peace?
3. What is the benefit of using technology in peacekeeping missions?

Unit 14 *Student B*

With a partner, complete this chart.

SDG	Goal	Action 1	Action 2
1	No Poverty		Donating clothing to people in need
2		Supporting local farmers	
3	Good Health and Well-being		Encouraging healthy eating habits
4		Donating school supplies to underprivileged students	
5	Gender Equality		Supporting equal pay for equal work
6		Using eco-friendly cleaning products	
7	Affordable and Clean Energy		Reducing the use of fossil fuels
8		Supporting local businesses that provide good working conditions	
9	Industry, Innovation and Infrastructure		Supporting companies that use sustainable manufacturing

■ Useful phrases

"What is the goal of SDG 2 ?"

"What is an action of SDG 2 ?"

"If we support local farmers, which SDG are we helping?

"How do you spell encouraging?"

"How do you say supporting in Japanese?"

Reading Log

You can use this sheet to record your reading times for each unit in the book. Reading is a skill that takes practice!

	Attempt									
Unit	1	2	3	4	5	6	7	8	9	10
1										
2										
3										
4										
6										
7										
8										
9										
11										
12										
13										
14										

Our World Tomorrow: How technology will change our lives
英語で学ぶ地球の未来とSDGs —クリティカル・シンキングを養う総合英語 [B-961]

1 刷 2024年2月14日

著 者	マレー・アダム	Adam Murray
	パッソス・アンデルソン	Anderson Passos
発行者	南雲一範 Kazunori Nagumo	
発行所	株式会社 南雲堂 〒162-0801 東京都新宿区山吹町361 NAN'UN-DO Co., Ltd. 361 Yamabuki-cho, Shinjuku-ku, Tokyo 162-0801, Japan 振替口座：00160-0-46863 TEL: 03-3268-2311（営業部：学校関係） 03-3268-2384（営業部：書店関係） 03-3268-2387（編集部） FAX: 03-3269-2486	
編集者	加藤 敦	
表 紙	銀月堂	
組 版	Office haru	
検 印	省 略	
コード	ISBN978-4-523-17961-0 C0082	

Printed in Japan

E-mail nanundo@post.email.ne.jp
URL https://www.nanun-do.co.jp/